Memoir of Harlan Page

"Here, a child, I sinned and strayed;
"Here, the Savior disobeyed;
"Here, I felt his chast'ning rod;
"Here, I trust, returned to God."

Impromptu in an Album. Page 94.

MEMOIR OF HARLAN PAGE

The Power of Prayer and Personal Effort for the Souls of Individuals

BY

WILLIAM A. HALLOCK

Late Corresponding Secretary of the American Tract Society

CURIOSMITH

MINNEAPOLIS

2012

Published by Curiosmith.
P. O. Box 390293, Minneapolis, Minnesota, 55439, USA.
Internet: curiosmith.com.
E-mail: shopkeeper@curiosmith.com.

Previously published by the AMERICAN TRACT SOCIETY in 1835.

ISBN 9781935626640

CONTENTS

CHAPTER 1—INTRODUCTORY—(PAGE 9)—Importance of personal effort and prayer for *individuals*—Christian influence not brought *into contact* with men—a principle of the Divine economy—inculcated by Christ and the Apostles, and by examples of eminent Christians—object of this memoir.

CHAPTER 2—FIVE YEARS RESIDENCE IN HIS NATIVE PLACE FROM THE TIME OF HIS CONVERSION—(PAGE 12)—His birth—marriage—conversion—appeal to a hardened sinner—severe illness—letters to an awakened sinner—her conversion—directions for Christian duty—letter to one in affliction—various efforts—reflections on a Sabbath—letter to a young man—resolutions to be active—evidences of good—conversion of the young man above addressed—letter to an impenitent acquaintance—warning to a young lady against enticing company—laments his deadness in religion—letter to an impenitent relative—letter from an awakened sinner—his reply—new resolution to be faithful—several awakened—solemn appeal to the impenitent printed as cards—letter to a late pupil—letter from one awakened, and reply—letter to a cousin in the state of New York—his conversion.

CHAPTER 3—RESIDENCE OF TWO MONTHS IN BOSTON, AND NEARLY THREE YEARS IN COVENTRY—(PAGE 34)—Letters from Boston—visits churches and Sabbath schools there—church music—Rev. Levi Parsons—monthly concert—death-bed of a Universalist—settlement of a pastor in Coventry—laments his want of spirituality—interesting visit in a revival of religion—work of grace in Coventry—letter to one persisting in sin—to an esteemed friend not pious—to a young lady—motives to early piety—letter to a young convert—extensive revivals—letter to a young lady, and reply—letter to a relative—letter to an "almost Christian."

CHAPTER 4—RESIDENCE OF TWO MONTHS IN JEWETT CITY, AND EIGHTEEN MONTHS IN COVENTRY—(PAGE 47)—Journey to Jewett City—efforts in a family and factory on the way—visit to a school-house—sense of responsibility—commences a prayer-meeting on Wednesday evenings and on Sabbath mornings at sunrise—visit to a sick man—efforts for thoughtless youth—monthly concert—questions his motives—Sabbath school gathered—prayer-meeting of teachers—increase of Sabbath school—several seriously impressed—conversions—letter to a gentleman—books lent—summary view of his usefulness in Jewett City—compelled by ill health to return to Coventry—unable to converse, but writes to one resisting the Spirit—narrative of conversation with a young lady on dancing, etc.—her conversion—letter to a young lady on professing Christ—to a young lady on the death of a friend—to a young gentleman—a desperate effort for one who still delayed repentance—outpouring of the Spirit—his abundant labors—testimonies to his fidelity.

CHAPTER 5—HIS NARRATIVE OF THOMAS HAMITAH PATOO, A NATIVE OF THE MARQUESAS ISLANDS, HOPEFULLY BROUGHT TO CHRIST IN COVENTRY—(Page 62)—Thomas steals away from his father and embarks in an American ship—is found in Boston by a benevolent individual and placed in Coventry—becomes anxious for his soul—his conversion, as narrated by himself—his anxiety for the impenitent—urgent entreaties to a delaying sinner—and to one now in the ministry—Mr. Page accompanies him to the Foreign Mission school in Cornwall—his letter to Mr. Page—death.

CHAPTER 6—CLOSE OF HIS LABORS IN COVENTRY—(Page 68)—Severe sickness—engages in engraving—letter describing the Missionary museum at Andover—to a young lady—to one who had given up her hope—testimony of his pastor and other individuals—gratifying results—faithful efforts being by some perverted no valid objection.

CHAPTER 7—FROM THE TIME OF HIS CONNECTION WITH THE AMERICAN TRACT SOCIETY TO THE REVIVAL OF 1831, EMBRACING THE PERIOD OF THE SIGNAL DISPLAYS OF DIVINE GRACE IN THE TRACT AND BIBLE HOUSES—(Page 75)—Constant pressure of duty—superintends a large Sabbath school of boys—conversions in his Sabbath school and in the congregation—interesting work of grace in the Tract and Bible houses—boldness of infidelity—exertions for supplying the destitute of the city—concern for the salvation of his children—conversion of a friend residing in his family—anonymous note to a skillful player on the piano—consecrated as an officer of the church—request for the services of his former pastor—ardent hopes for our country—letter of thanks from a teacher of his Sabbath school, then in college—letter to his sister—to afflicted relatives—communication for London—history of the revival in Tract and Bible houses—letter from a fellow-laborer—cheering results—conversions—letter to a bereaved brother—encouragement to a missionary—commencement of systematic Christian effort connected with Tract distribution—its usefulness—brief and severe illness—son and daughter unite with the church.

CHAPTER 8—FROM THE COMMENCEMENT OF THE REVIVAL OF 1831 TO HIS LAST SICKNESS, EMBRACING RESULTS OF HIS SABBATH SCHOOL, HIS SUPERINTENDENCE OF CHRISTIAN EFFORT CONNECTED WITH TRACT DISTRIBUTION, AND THE TRANSFER OF HIS LABORS TO A NEW CHURCH— (PAGE 90)—Wonderful effusions of the Holy Spirit—encouragement to praying parents—usefulness of a letter to a friend in Boston—his burning zeal and incessant efforts—failure of health—resigns superintendence of Sabbath school—most gratifying results—visits Coventry—sketch of his father's house—counsel to his son on entering an academy—instructs a female Bible class—superintends Christian effort connected with Tract distribution in 14th ward—means to secure direct efforts for the salvation of individuals—success of his own efforts in a district—labors during the prevalence of cholera—communication to a meeting of his Tract distributors—to the female Bible class—letter to his parents—to his son—Tract distributors' day of fasting—interesting family scene—transfer to a new church—closes his connection with Tract distribution in 14th ward— results—testimony of the pastor of the church he left—superintends a new Sabbath school—decline of health—letters to his son and daughter—testimony of the preacher at the new church—last item of business.

CHAPTER 9—PROMINENT CHARACTERISTICS OF HIS EFFORTS FOR THE SALVATION OF MEN—(PAGE 107)—It was the burden of his heart—list of names—efforts unremitted—waking in tears—object not to be happy, but useful—felt necessity to all of being "born again"—anecdote of a young merchant—labored for individuals—followed up impressions made—clear sense of obligation—appeal to a Christian who watched with him—a farewell message—labored to bring men to a decision, illustrated by two anecdotes and a letter—expected success from God in answer to prayer—prayed much—character of his prayers—effect on himself— obtained premium Tract on prayer—acknowledged perfect obligation and perfect dependence—uniform and unwearied—spirituality of religion not to be excluded from social meetings—fruitfulness in expedients for doing good—as the father of a family—letter from his son—paragraphs for religious papers—album—Temperance cause—young men directed to the ministry—did not live to accumulate property—anecdote—skill in selecting Tracts—all the efficiency of God—great blessing of his labors—testimony on his death-bed—powerful influence of such a life for the conversion of the world.

CHAPTER 10—TRIUMPHS OF GRACE ON HIS DYING BED— (PAGE 115)—His certainty of his departure for many weeks—clear state of mind—reception of the announcement that he must die—seeks continual presence of Christ—not obtained for some days—new view of his love— how obtained—love of the brethren—and of souls—affecting conversation with the author—gratitude for mercies—sense of unworthiness—commits his family to God—no more concern about his burial—messages to his parents and friends in Coventry—longs to depart—ascribes all his usefulness to divine grace—deep sense of sin—delightful anticipation of heaven— relishes only what is spiritual—portions of the Bible and Hymns—urges Christians to duty—longs for a spirit of love in the churches—utterance in disturbed sleep—visit of a fellow-laborer—influence of sacred music in the chamber of death—hymns "Rock of Ages," and "My Faith Looks Up to Thee"—portions of other precious hymns—importance of cultivating sacred music—instrumental music—tenderness of spirit—gratitude to his physician—exhorts his companion to trust in God—anecdotes illustrating his dread of sin and sense of unworthiness—arrival of his son—prayers— dying messages to his family—commits them and himself to God—subscription for his family—anecdote—his grave.

CHAPTER 1

INTRODUCTORY.

Faithful Christian Biography has at once its sanction and model in the word of God; and in our own times, its excellent practical influence is confirmed in the history of many eminent individuals. Most of these, by their superior talents, education, or commanding spheres of action, present an example which the community in general may indeed *admire*, but which few, comparatively, can hope to *imitate*.

The present unpretending memoir exhibits the fidelity and success of a humble Christian, whose opportunities and powers were scarcely superior to those of thousands; and is chiefly designed to illustrate a single point—THE POWER OF PRAYER AND PERSONAL EFFORT FOR THE SOULS OF INDIVIDUALS.

It is obvious to all, that the kingdom of Christ can be extended in our world only by the accession of *individuals*. His blood avails not to the salvation of men *in the mass;* but to those who *individually* repent of sin, and accept of his mercy. The Holy Spirit strives with men and sanctifies them *only as individuals*. It is as *individuals* that the inhabitants of our world must be raised to heaven, or sink to hell. Yet to how great an extent are the prayers and contributions of Christians made indefinitely for the conversion of the world *as a whole*, while the salvation of *no one individual* is the object of their *personal* and persevering endeavors! How great a portion of that "light of the world," which the church is commanded to reflect, is so "hid," that no one individual sees it and feels its influence! how great a portion of the "salt of the earth," by which men are to be purified and saved, is so kept in the mass, as to be brought **into contact** with none!

The truth evidently is, that *personal efforts for the souls of individuals*—the lip, and thoughts and heart of a living man, brought into contact with the lip, and thoughts and heart of a living man—is *a grand institution of God* for the conversion of the world; and we must expect success, not in neglecting, but in coinciding with the Divine economy. It was when "they that feared the Lord *spake often one to another*," that his book of remembrance was written. His command is, "As every man hath received the gift, even so *minister the same one to another*." Not only "the Spirit and the Bride," but *"he that heareth"* must "say, come." Christians are exhorted to "shine as lights in the world, *holding forth the word of life;*" and the blessed encouragement is given, "He which converteth the sinner from the error of his way shall save a soul from death, and hide a multitude of sins." The parable of Nathan illustrates this principle with inimitable force and beauty: *"Thou* art the man," humbled the king in the dust before God.

The same principle is exemplified in the success of the personal efforts of the pious mother; of the skillful Sabbath School and Bible Class instructor; and of faithful pastoral visitation: in all which Divine truth is happily pressed upon the heart of the individual. It has also an irresistible confirmation in the fact, that WHEREVER the Holy Spirit is largely poured out, the ministers and members of the church abound in faithful conversation and prayer with each other, and with the impenitent.

Much of the "preaching" of the New Testament was unquestionably of this sort. To such labor were the apostles sent out by our Savior, who sanctioned his instructions by his own divine example.

Paul, with all his crushing public responsibilities, could testify to the Ephesian elders, that he had labored among them both "publicly and from house to house;" and appeal to them as witnesses of his own fidelity, in the memorable and most emphatic words: "REMEMBER, THAT, BY THE SPACE OF THREE YEARS, I CEASED NOT TO WARN EVERY ONE, NIGHT AND DAY, WITH TEARS."

By such labor preeminently have *pagans* and *men far from God,* in all circumstances and periods of time, been brought to attend on the public means of grace, and join themselves to his people.

Of the signal outpouring of the Holy Spirit among the natives of Ceylon, in connection with the American mission, the REV. MR. WINSLOW states, that "there were few cases of permanent conviction, in which religious impressions were not cherished by much patient labor of the missionaries or their assistants, in *conversing and praying with individuals alone.* It was this *repeated and personal* application of truth, which principally took effect."

This class of effort was a grand means of the unparalleled success of the ministry of BAXTER at Kidderminster.

"If I had true love to souls," said HENRY MARTYN, when contemplating a foreign mission, "I should *long and labor for those around me,* and afterwords for the conversion of the heathen;" and often did he "redeem time from study, from recreation, and from the intercourse of friends, that he might enter the abodes of misery, to arose the unthinking slumberer, or administer consolation to the dejected penitent."

"Our views," said James Brainerd Taylor, when a student in college, must "not be confined to the end of our preparatory course. There are many opportunities *now* of doing good. *The call from many a lowly cottage is, 'Come over and help us.'*" Again: "Resolved that I will, the Lord being my helper, think, speak and act as an *individual;* for as such I must live, as such I must die, stand before God, and be damned or saved for ever and ever. I have been waiting for others: I must act as if I were the only one to act, and wait no longer."

If adding another example of the steadfastness of aim, self-denying perseverance, skill, and success with which a humble Christian discharged the same duty—connected, through the grace of God, with a most blessed and triumphant death—shall have any influence in encouraging other Christians thus to labor for God and the souls of men, the publication of this little work will not be in vain.

It is proper the reader should be informed that there does not appear the slightest indication that the subject of this sketch anticipated the publication of any memorial of himself. Of many of the most interesting scenes of his life he left no record whatever, except incidentally in hasty letters to his friends—evidently so intent on securing the *results* as to forget the *record* of them, or so constantly occupied as to have no time to prepare it. Almost all his communications here inserted have been abridged and condensed, with slight changes in the phraseology, while the sentiment is scrupulously retained.

CHAPTER 2

FIVE YEARS RESIDENCE IN HIS NATIVE PLACE FROM
THE TIME OF HIS CONVERSION.

HARLAN PAGE was born in Coventry, in the county of Tolland,
Connecticut, July 28, 1791. He was the only son of pious parents;
always sustained a good moral character; was taught by his father the trade
of a house-joiner, and received a good common education.

In May, 1813, he married Miss MARY KINGSBURY, who was to be the
helper of his spiritual course till his death, though at the time of their marriage neither of them were pious. The earliest letter written by him, which
has come to hand, is the following, addressed to Rev. E. T. W——, who was
then his minister.

"*Sabbath morning, Oct.* 17, 1813.

"REV. AND DEAR SIR,—Your prayers, I trust, have been heard. My dear
companion hopes she has accepted of the Savior, and devoted herself and her
all to him. But I am yet in the gall of bitterness, in opposition to God—my
anguish last night was almost insupportable. I could see my Savior nailed to
the cross, bleeding and dying for sinners. I could see him with open arms,
saying, 'Come unto me, all ye that labor and are heavy laden, and I will give
you rest.' I could pray, but this only increased my pain. I fear the Holy Spirit
will leave me to hardness of heart and blindness of mind. O do remember
me in your prayers; for the prayer of faith availeth much.

"Your affectionate and distressed friend,

"HARLAN PAGE"

His distress for his sins was such at this period, that he frequently left
his work to retire and pray; and as he rode to and from a neighboring town
where he was engaged in business, he often felt constrained to stop and go
into the grove to plead for mercy. He soon engaged in instructing a school,

where, after dismissing his pupils, he often remained for meditation and prayer. He was thus engaged in solitude one evening, when his sense of his lost condition as a sinner became so intense that he felt that he could not again leave the throne of grace till the controversy with his Maker was closed. There, in the darkness of midnight, and under the guidance, none can doubt, of the Holy Spirit, he consecrated himself to his Redeemer: not merely in the confidence of pardon and acceptance, but with the determination to live and labor to promote his glory in the salvation of the perishing. "When I first obtained a hope," he said on his dying bed, "I felt that *I must labor for souls. I prayed, year after year, that God would make me the means of saving souls.*"

On Sabbath, March 6, 1814, he and his companion, with twenty others, publicly professed their faith in Christ, and joined the visible church.

Only three days after this we find the date of an interesting and faithful letter, addressed to a relative who had long been hardening himself in sin and resisting the strivings of the Holy Spirit. He seems to suppose his friend to be perverting the doctrine of his dependence upon God, as an excuse for willfully continuing in sin. He first quotes the objection as it is strongly stated by Baxter in his Call to the Unconverted, together with the whole of Baxter's reply. He then presses the same considerations in his own language, supporting them by numerous commands and promises from the Bible, and adds:

"Were you in a boat just above an awful cataract, already feeling the force of the impetuous current, would you not endeavor to reach the shore? Would you say, 'I can do nothing: God must save me without my own exertions, if I am saved at all?' Why then will you not strive to escape a more terrible destruction—the eternal, inconceivable horrors of a lost soul?

"You allow that a change of heart is necessary; and will not be offended with my plainness. Could I but see you earnestly engaged for your salvation, how would my heart beat for joy; how would I give thanks to the eternal God!

"Dear Sir, do consider and picture to yourself the dying hour. Then you must see your danger. Will you then say that, when in health, you could not attend to the salvation of the soul? Will you not rather exclaim, 'O that I had a few days more to live, that I might prepare to die?'

"Do not say you cannot pray. Do you believe in the joys of heaven and the torments of despair; and will you not so much as ask God to grant you the one, and save you from the other? Turning away from God and heaven, I am sure your own reason must convict you of madness and awful presumption.

"Your affectionate friend,

"H. PAGE"

In the summer of this year God saw fit to discipline his servant by a very severe, protracted and painful illness, by which he was brought to hold intimate converse with death, and taught to sympathize with the suffering. His sickness is thus described in a letter to an aunt, dated, Coventry, October 18, 1814.

"About the 20th of May I was attacked with fever, which continued two or three weeks; and left me with an affection of the liver, attended with severe pain, which baffled the skill of physicians. It continued for eleven weeks, when a swelling began to rise on my back, which was exceedingly painful, and was at length opened by Dr. W——, who was obliged to make a deep and long incision in the live flesh. I have been chiefly confined to my bed for seventeen weeks."

To another friend he writes: *"Experience*, more than observation, I find, teaches our need of Divine support in affliction. With it, we can endure the most piercing pain, and rejoice with thankfulness; and even in the immediate prospect of death, no terror alarms. The spirit, in a near view of eternal glory, forgets the pain, and longs to soar on high."

The grand lesson, which he felt that this sickness taught him, was that he must devote the life God had preserved more faithfully to him, in labors for the salvation of all to whom he had access.

His next letter which has come to hand was addressed to a pious female relative who was *walking in spiritual darkness*, designed to aid her in self-examination. He inquires whether she had neglected prayer, indulged in any known sin, been remiss in efforts for the spiritual welfare of those around her, or in any known duty; and entreats her to return to her heavenly Father, and consecrate herself anew to him, assured that his grace should be sufficient for her.

The next is to a young lady who had been *under serious impressions* while a member of his school, urging her not to delay repentance, but come with all her heart and embrace the Savior.

The next to a young friend who had professed Christ, but was *exposed to temptations* from thoughtless companions.

The next, bearing date September 3, 1815, is addressed to one who was a playmate of his childhood, but of whose conversion he had heard at M——, N. Y. requesting a particular account of his religious exercises, and especially that he would *address a letter* to his former acquaintance in Coventry who continued out of Christ, and remember them in his prayers.

"Since you were here," he says, "we have been visited with the gracious outpouring of the Spirit, and nearly fifty have been added to the church; but alas! there are yet many promising youth who neglect offered mercy; and who, if sovereign grace do not interpose, must sink into unending wo.

I doubt not you feel how great is their danger, and long for their salvation. Do write to them; it may be God will make you the instrument of salvation to their souls. They respect you, and should you address them, they may listen to your warnings and come to Christ. Do also pray for us and them. God is every where present, and will hear the prayer of faith."

Two days after, we find a letter addressed to E. L———, a young lady for whose salvation he had labored during her residence of a few days in his family, and who was under the *strivings of the Holy Spirit.*

"The language of Jehovah is, 'the soul that sinneth, it shall die.' There is not one of Adam's lost race who has not forfeited eternal life by his sins. But there is one refuge, and one alone. Jesus Christ can save us; and he is ready to receive every returning sinner, and make him an heir of eternal joy. Sleep not, E———, take no rest, day nor night, till you have obtained peace with God. The billows of his wrath roll just beneath the steps of all the unconverted. Delay not a moment. No future time can be more favorable. Call upon God without ceasing; and if you perish, perish pleading for mercy. Let nothing divert your attention. If you grieve the Holy Spirit, his gracious influences may never return; and you (O overwhelming thought!) must sink where hope can never come; where mercy never gains admission. A few Christian friends are praying for you daily. Nothing but love impels me to write. Will you inform me what progress you are making, and what are your unshaken resolutions?

"With affection and esteem,

"H. Page"

TO THE SAME.

"Monday evening, Sept. 11, 1815.

"Friend E———, Are you yet without hope? Gloomy and dejected, do you yet go mourning, without one ray of heavenly grace? If so, your situation is trying; but I trust you would not for worlds return to your former state of thoughtlessness. You say you desire more pungent and heart-piercing convictions—to be awakened from your dangerous stupidity. Call upon God to place your sins before you; to humble you in the dust for them; and to show mercy to a guilty, repenting, returning prodigal. All you have to do is to cast yourself unreservedly, with all your sins, upon the mercy of Christ; to be deeply humbled for them; and with faith in the Redeemer's blood, take him as your only hope and portion. Never can you make yourself more acceptable to him. He only can clothe you with his own righteousness. He is ready to receive you. Go then, dear friend, in the best manner you are able, and cast yourself into his arms with all your guilt.

'There is a mercy-seat,
'Sprinkled with blood, where Jesus answers prayer;
'There humbly cast yourself beneath his feet,
'For never needy sinner perished there.'

"Beware of every sin. Cling not to your thoughtless companions. If you will serve God, you must expect the neglect and reproaches of some of them. But who are they? Are they the truly wise? Are they truly happy? Are they safe? Alas! they are on the brink of perdition.

"Faint not, while you have life. Fear not enemies. Fight the warfare of faith, and you shall win the glorious inheritance of the blessed.

"With affectionate regard, your friend,

"H. PAGE"

The result of these faithful efforts, through the divine blessing, may be gathered from the following extract of a letter to a Christian friend, dated,

Monday, sunset, Oct. 30, 1815.

"I have joyful news to tell you—news which has made heaven glad. Our friend E—— appears to be enjoying as much happiness as mortals are allowed this side of eternity. 'O,' says she, (in a letter she had just written him, with an overflowing heart) 'the height and depth of the love of Christ! How precious does this dear Savior now appear to me! Tongue can never express, nor heart conceive, which has not experienced the same, the sweet peace and joy I have found in him.'"

In a subsequent letter to Mr. Page, she says, "Your first epistle found me in the gall of bitterness; and but for your friendly advice, I fear I should now have been pursuing the vanities of the world. The Savior was pleased to make you the happy instrument of showing me my sins, and bringing me to partake of his love."

His own *views of Christian duty* at this time may be gathered from the following extract of a letter addressed to this young convert, November 16.

"Let us, E——, cast our eyes around on the poor, thoughtless, dying impenitent. How should we supplicate the throne of grace in their behalf! But this is not all. We must tell them of their danger, and point them to a bleeding Savior.

"An excuse is made by many Christians, which I conceive will not bear the scrutiny of the judgment day: they say they *have not the talents* for addressing the impenitent and conversing with them on the subject of religion. But are the simple truths of the Gospel so dark, that only the learned can understand them? Are the words, 'He that believeth shall be saved, but he that believeth not shall be damned,' so obscure, that we cannot properly impress them upon others? Is the road to perdition so plainly described in the Bible, and can we raise no warning voice to the throngs who travel it? Are the happiness of the righteous and the everlasting torments of the impenitent so clearly described, and can we see friends around us crowding their way to despair, with our lips closed in perpetual silence? The truth is, our faith in eternal realities is weak, and our sense of duty faint, while we thus neglect the salvation of our fellow-beings. Let us awake to duty; and while we have a tongue or pen, devote them to the service of the Most High, not in our own strength, but with strong faith and confidence in him."

Two days after, we find him attempting to lead the mind of a young lady to *improve the death of a beloved father* to her own spiritual good.

"The recent afflictive event and an earnest desire for your eternal salvation constitute all the apology I need offer for now addressing you. But what shall I say? Whom am I addressing? a humble follower of the blessed Jesus, or one who has no interest in him? If the former, how happy are you! If the latter, how awful, how tremendous are the divine denunciations against you, unless you renounce the world and accept of offered mercy! Of late you have abundantly needed some kind hand to support you.

"Were your beloved father to speak to you from another world, how impressive would be his language! Would he say, 'Sleep on: forget a dying hour: regard not the threatenings of Jehovah: let this world be your portion?' No; he would rather say, 'Neglect not the calls of mercy. Sleep not upon the brink of perdition. Awake! arise! prepare to meet your God! Delay not; for the day of the Lord is at hand.' While on the bed of death, he uttered, in broken accents, the words, 'Repent, repent.' May this providence lead you faithfully to examine your heart, and see if you are prepared to follow him. God's design in this affliction is doubtless that you may come to him as the only source of real consolation; that you may be humble, and prayerful, and better fitted to be useful in life and happy in heaven. May you all have divine support. Accept these lines as an expression of affection and sympathy, and an earnest desire that they may be instrumental of some good to your immortal soul.

"With esteem, your friend,

"H. PAGE"

Four days after, we find a full letter addressed to a Christian friend, on the duty of *faithful self-examination,* with a scriptural view of the more palpable and decisive tests of Christian character.

Early in December he commenced a letter to his Christian brother at M——, N.Y. which shows the deep interest he then felt in the spiritual

welfare of many individuals, as well as of the church generally. He com-
plains of his own languid affections; states that there were then no revivals
of religion in all the eastern portion of the State; that Christians generally seemed to have become languid and formal, and the impenitent to be
"unconcerned, while the wrath of heaven is impending over them."

"R——," he says, "when in conversation, pleads, as do many others,
the ungodly lives of professors of religion. He 'rather thinks that, if he lives
a moral life and prays in secret, he is on the road to heaven as well as many
who make so much ado about religion.'

"As to Mrs. ——, I am not now particularly acquainted with the state
of her mind. She is very reserved in conversation on the subject of religion,
as are many others of the unconverted, and even many who profess to be
the disciples of Christ. How criminal is our neglect to improve every proper
opportunity in conversing on the most important of all subjects!

"L—— S—— read your letter, but seems not deeply affected with his
lost condition as a sinner. His wife, in the late revival, almost ventured to
indulge a hope; but she is now more reserved on religious subjects."

This gentleman used to complain of the visits of his wife at the house
of Mr. Page; as he said she always returned "in such a fever about her soul;"
but both ere long had a new song put into their mouths.

"A—— P——" (proceeds the letter) "gives his assent to the truths of
religion; but argues, that if he attends on the public means of grace, he commits more sin than if he stays at home; and asks how he can pray, when he
has not the least inclination to the duty.

"I feel greatly condemned for not making more faithful efforts for the
salvation of these dear friends.

"E——, (above alluded to,) has lately been brought to experience the
boundless love of the Savior, and her happiness in him seems to be almost
without alloy. At our next communion she expects publicly to devote herself to him.

"Since I commenced this letter we have established a weekly prayer-
meeting. The first meeting was remarkably well attended. A few individuals
seem to be aroused, and the prospect seems a little more favorable. I beg
your prayers for us as a people, and for

"Your unworthy and affectionate brother,

"H. PAGE"

The following is an anonymous note, in which he *enclosed an appropriate Tract* to a young man, by whose profaneness he had been recently
pained, on meeting him at a public store.

"Accept the inclosed from one who earnestly desires your best good;

and may I beg the favor that you will read it with candor, and weigh well the sentiments it contains. I have seen you only once; but then had reason to fear that you have not seriously considered the sin of taking the name of that God in vain, in whose hand is your life, and who alone can save you from eternal wo. My sense of your danger was such that I could not refrain from addressing you and entreating you to turn to God and live.

"Affectionately your

"FELLOW TRAVELLER TO ETERNITY"

Under date of June 9, 1816, he writes as follows: "Though detained, in the providence of God, from his house this day, my heart is still there. I anticipate with pleasure and joy the visitation of the Spirit of grace among this people. I almost imagine I now see the tear of the guilty penitent, and hear the language of the heart, in broken accents, 'What must I do to be saved?' Are not God's children engaged? Are not their united prayers now ascending, an acceptable sacrifice to an almighty Savior?

"O God, hear our united cry for mercy on perishing sinners. Help us to abase ourselves before thee, and in faith plead for the outpouring of the Spirit, to awaken thy children, and convict and convert the impenitent. May our assembly be clothed in sackcloth for our sins; sighs break from broken hearts, and hundreds be new clothed with the spotless robe of our Savior's righteousness. Encourage the heart of our minister by shaking these dry bones, and raising up multitudes as champions for the truth as it is in Jesus. Let thy power be made known in all the churches, and spread thy blessing abroad in the earth, till the reign of our exalted God and King shall be universal."

"*Coventry, June* 15, 1816.
To E—— L——, (the young lady addressed Sept. 11, 1815.)

"Yesterday I attended a prayer-meeting at a school-house in T——. As I entered, the very sight of the people thrilled through my soul. More than 200 were assembled in deep solemnity. Some, slain by the law, seemed to say in agony of soul, 'I must die, and lie down in eternal sorrow. I am at enmity with God. Wo is me; I perish. Lord God, have mercy, have mercy.' The work is apparently progressing. Rev. Mr. N—— informed me that between sixty and seventy have hopefully been born again, and that about an equal number are under conviction of sin. What a glorious display of Divine grace and mercy!

"I rejoice that you have tokens of the Divine favor in A——. When reading your letter, sensations not to be described arose in my breast; and a renewed resolution to devote myself more entirely to God was, I trust, the happy effect. But yet *of one thing I stand in fear*—that, should God see fit to make me the instrument of good to any soul, I shall not give him all the glory. *O for that humility, which God approves, and which makes man useful to man!* Much do I need it. May God help me to obtain it.

"There are two or three instances of conviction among us—I hope as happy preludes to a general outpouring of the Spirit.

"I shall write a few lines to S——, at your request. You have opportunities of conversing with him. *Don't let them slip.* Warn him to flee from the wrath to come, and fly to Jesus for safety.

"Yours sincerely,

"H. Page"

To the young man alluded to in the last paragraph, he wrote as follows:

"Dear Sir,—Understanding that you have been led to discover the necessity of religion, I have presumed (though unacquainted with you) to write you a few lines. You are sensible that there is a God; that by his holy law the soul that sins must die; and that all men have broken this law, and are exposed to his just indignation through the countless ages of eternity. O, sir, (for you will suffer me to speak freely,) are you of this number? Do you stand on the borders of eternal wo—'where their worm dieth not and the fire is not quenched?' But stop—the contemplation strikes horror into the soul. Let us view the enrapturing scene of redeeming love. Souls that have sinned are not altogether hopeless. When all were condemned by sin, then it was that the Lord Jesus gave himself an offering—bare our sins—and suffered the inexpressible agonies of death, that we, poor guilty rebels, might have life. This blessed Savior is ready to receive you. My young friend, 'all things are ready.' Cast yourself, just as you are, on him for pardon, sanctification and salvation. Delay not. While you delay you aggravate your guilt. Call on God day and night; search the Scriptures; and let not your reluctant heart prove your ruin for ever. Death may be near. Resolve, if you perish, to perish pleading for mercy. I entreat you delay not; but this moment go to Christ and 'take of the waters of life freely.'

"With sincere regard, your friend,

"H. Page"

On the following day he wrote to C——, a young female friend with whom he had long been intimate, a letter full of moving and earnest entreaty to attend to the concerns of her soul; and requesting her to communicate it to a female acquaintance, and converse freely with her on the great subject it brought before them.

In a memorandum of the same date he expresses some concern in respect to his health, which he had not entirely recovered since his severe illness, and as to the means of supporting his family; but resigns all to the will of God.

"That my life is not to be a long one," he adds, "some monitor within seems frequently to tell me, which I hope may incite me to greater diligence in duty, and continual preparation for eternity. O Lord, do thou direct me in the right way. Be my guide in every concern of life. Let me not do any thing from false motives. *Keep me constantly humble and constantly engaged for the good of all souls around me.* Grant that my companion and myself may zealously cooperate in every good work; never distrust thy providence: and be guided where we may be shining lights, and be useful. Should our dear babe be left fatherless or motherless, do thou provide for it; preserve his life; renew his heart; and make him the means of salvation to many souls through Emmanuel's name.

"H. Page"

The following memorandum, dated July 4, contains an intimation that God was blessing his efforts, and that he ascribed to him all the glory.

"Shall I ever have cause to regret addressing some of my fellow-men by letter on the concerns of eternity? Will not the blessing God has seen fit to grant on some of my endeavors, prevent all regret in this or the future world? Shall not the *conversion* of souls, of which I have just had intelligence, stimulate me to more active endeavors to be useful to man, and to honor my divine Master? To him belongs all the glory. God forbid that I should take any of it to myself. What am I?—a vile reptile of the earth, just crawling on the brink of the grave."

"Coventry, July 8, 1816.

To E—— L——,

"Persevere, Eliza, in the good work. Use all your influence. Warn those around you, with discretion and prudence, and your crown of rejoicing shall receive additional lustre in the great day of the Lord.

"You ask what are our prospects. We don't yet despair. Some Christians are uncommonly engaged, and some youth are serious. F—— W—— appears to be under deep conviction. G—— and her sister I—— are anxiously inquiring what they must do to be saved."

July 8, having heard glad tidings from S——, the young man whom he addressed June 15, he wrote him as follows:

"Monday, P. M. July, 1816.

"Dear Sir,—In imagination I cordially take you by the hand, and call you Brother. Happy are you, if the allurements of the world have lost their charms; and Christ, as you hope, has made you an heir of glory. You have entered on a warfare; and though the enemy may not now be in full view, you will need to be clad with the whole armor of God to resist his wiles.

"Go on and rejoice. Do much for the cause of Christ. Be diligent in duty, and neglect not to warn your companions in sin. Be prudent; discreet; guard against temptation; be affectionate to your companions; let your example be upright, always trusting in God for assistance in every thing you do. I wish to write more, but cannot add now.

"With sincere affection, your friend,

"H. PAGE"

How must our departed brother's heart have been cheered by receiving the following reply from this young friend, whose face, when he first addressed him, he had never seen!

"DEAR SIR,—The name of Brother, by which you were pleased to call me, endeared you to my heart, though I feel unworthy to be called by that name. O Sir, what a deplorable condition was I in! I was fighting against God and sporting with eternal realities; and should have remained so till death, had not Almighty love snatched me from the pit of destruction. O wondrous love indeed manifested to my soul! I think I am now enabled to view, by faith, the 'Lamb of God who taketh away the sin of the world.' The Sabbath after I saw you, the load of guilt was, I trust, removed from my heart, and before I was aware, I was praising God. O why did Jesus snatch me thus from everlasting burnings!

"Twas the same love that spread the feast,
  "That sweetly forced me in;
"Else I had still refused to taste,
  "And perished in my sin."

"O that I may be enabled to do something for God—something for that dear Redeemer who bled, and groaned, and died on Calvary for one so guilty as I.

"O Sir, you cannot imagine how much I desire to see you. Will you not still continue to write me? *Your letters were the means of awakening me to the concerns of my soul.* When I first heard them read, horror seized my mind; I was brought to see myself a guilty sinner, justly condemned by the holy law of God. E—— L——, after conversing solemnly with me one evening, read several of your letters. I never shall forget the impression they made upon my mind, and also *upon the minds of my two brothers;* for God was pleased to awaken us all at this time. O, Dear Sir, may God reward you for your love to immortal souls. *Do write to all the dear youth in Coventry.* Tell them from me, there is nothing but religion worth living for. Tell them the storm of Divine wrath is impending over them. Entreat them to fly to Jesus for safety, lest they hear his awful sentence, 'Depart, ye cursed, into everlasting fire.'

"Your affectionate, though unworthy friend,

"S—— H——"

The following was addressed to an impenitent acquaintance, who frequently came very secretly to converse with Mr. Page:

To S—— L——,

"DEAR SIR,—Though I have had no particular conversation with you for some time, I still earnestly desire to know the state of your mind. Have you yet no evidence that your peace is made with God, and are you still treasuring up wrath against the day of wrath? If so, let me beseech you, fly this moment and take refuge in the Savior. His ransom is sufficient for every returning prodigal.

"Do you wait to make yourself righteous? It is a visionary idea. In your own righteousness you can never proceed a step toward heaven. In vain will you wait in any way short of casting yourself unreservedly on the free grace and mercy of Christ. When you resolve in your own strength to live without sin, do you find you make any advances toward a pure and holy life? Are you not daily ensnared with temptations and easily besetting sins?

"Labor to view sin in all its deformity in the sight of God, and to get a thorough knowledge of your own heart. Repent of your sins. Read the Scriptures. Be constant and fervent in prayer, remembering for your encouragement, that 'the kingdom of heaven suffereth violence, and the violent take it by force.' Remember, that, while out of Christ, every moment is big with danger. Death is near. Eternity is near. Let me entreat you, lay hold on eternal life before it be for ever too late.

"With ardent desires for your salvation, your affectionate friend,

"H. PAGE"

"N. B. A few lines in return would be very gratifying."

"July 28, 1816. This day completes one fourth of a century of my life. More than twenty-two years have I lived in sin; less than three have I devoted, in any feeble measure, to the service of Christ. More than one third of 'threescore years and ten' is already elapsed, and probably more than one half of my life is spent. The grave must soon open for my body, and my soul be in eternity. May God make me faithful till death; and then, through boundless grace, receive me to glory."

To his friend at M——, N. Y. he says, under date of August 26, "Several towns in this vicinity have begun to experience refreshings from the presence of the Lord; and two young persons among us have lately been brought to rejoice in sovereign mercy, witnessing for God that we are not entirely forsaken. One is a daughter of Mr. H—— W——. The other, I know you will be rejoiced to hear, is Mrs. Z—— B——, who, within a few days, has a new song in her mouth, even praise to our God.

"I am told you have commenced study for the ministry. Is it so? It is a great work on which to enter to 'watch for souls;' but God's grace will aid all sincere endeavors to glorify him and save lost man. We expect to see you here this fall.

"Your friend and brother,

"H. PAGE"

"P. S. When you visit Coventry, I wish you to bring some of your favorite *church music.*"

To Mr. Page sacred music was, through life, a source of much religious enjoyment, and a constant auxiliary in family and social worship.

Having written a faithful letter to an estimable young female connection, endeavoring to induce her to separate herself from ungodly associates, he received a reply, inquiring what, in existing circumstances, she should do? His answer is as follows:

"*Saturday evening, March* 8, 1817.

"DEAR FRIEND,—As to the company at ——'s, I did not complain of your conduct there; but feared the consequences of frequenting such company. May I ask, Was God in all your thoughts? Did you speak a word for Christ? Did you obey the precept, 'Be not conformed to this world?'

"You ask, 'Must I not associate with any young people of my age?' I answer, do it just so far as you can and act the part of a decided Christian, or do good to souls. But when you find yourself overcome by temptation; indifferent to those follies and sins which once would have shocked you; violating your former resolutions, and with no evidence of benefit to your associates, wisdom and duty doubtless unite in deciding that you should break away from them without delay. A Christian must have uncommon grace in exercise, not to be injured by such company. And besides, it brings great reproach on religion. The world are keen-eyed to see the faults of Christians, and at once judge that, if they join in such amusements, their profession, is but hypocrisy.

"You have attended one such place of amusement; and can you reflect on it now with pleasure? Was it profitable to your soul? Suppose all the members of this church should join in a sleigh-ride, and tarry at a public house till midnight, partaking of the intoxicating bowl, and making merry with those around them—what would be said of religion? And why more improper for the whole than for one?

"I ask you again to consider that you are young, and may be drawn aside unawares. *In a time of such declension as the present, we are all in danger.* Consider how you would have viewed these things when you first felt the love of Christ in your heart.

"As ever, your friend,

"H. PAGE"

June 18, we find him thus writing bitter things against himself:

"Sabbath, P. M. 5 o'clock.

"Long have I neglected to record my religious exercises; and long have I lived, a formal professor of religion. I have forgotten my Savior, wandered from his sheep-fold, and grown unconcerned about my danger. While I write, I fear I have no true penitence. All is cold indifference and dead formality. The word of God is not to me a delight as it once was; its beauties are hid, and its promises and threatenings glided over unheeded and unapplied. I fear and believe this Sabbath has been improved by me to no spiritual advantage. Thus pass away my days, beclouded with sin, without engagedness in Zion's cause, without gratitude to my Savior, or obedience to his precepts.

"O thou blessed Jesus! I have forgotten thy love; have strayed from thee. I desire to humble myself with true repentance before thee. Help me to return from my backsliding; quicken me in duty; show me my ingratitude and my sins. May I fear to offend thee, and live henceforward to thy glory."

August 17, he thus addressed an impenitent female relative:

"DEAR SISTER,—I think much of you, and long to see you in the ark of safety. Have you reason to hope that your sins are pardoned through a Savior's blood? If not, consider your danger. O, Emeline, if you have not chosen God for your portion, you are every moment exposed to the torments of eternal despair. Should death now call you, you must sink 'where their worm dieth not, and the fire is not quenched.' Think, dear friend, of the sufferings of our ascended Lord. Think of his agony in the garden—how his head was pierced with thorns—how he was reviled by the multitude—how he was led to Calvary, and suspended, with nails driven through his hands and his feet, in agony, till he yielded up the ghost—and all this, dear sister, for such sinners as you and me.

"Shall we—will *you* despise this love and these sufferings? Death is coming apace. O delay not a moment to make preparation. Christ is ready to pardon every returning penitent—he is ready to receive and pardon *you*. Go then, as a weary and heavy laden sinner, implore his mercy, give yourself into his arms, and be happy for ever.

"Please to write your feelings. You need not fear to tell them to your affectionate friend, who earnestly longs for your happiness in this world and the world to come.

"H. PAGE"

Communications under date of January 30, 1818, mention that the Pastor of the church had been dismissed, leaving them without a spiritual guide; but state that the female members of the church were praying, and that two individuals were under deep convictions for sin.

The next communication is addressed to a pious friend, endeavoring to impart consolation under the partial loss of health, and accompanied by fifty Tracts for distribution.

The next to an impenitent acquaintance, who in sickness had been alarmed for his spiritual state, begging him to listen to this call from God, and portraying the infinite hazard of returning again to sin and folly.

The next is an awakening appeal to a young lady; and its influence may be inferred from the following reply, which is given as an example of the state of mind of some of the individuals whose eternal welfare pressed upon our brother's heart.

"*Coventry, March* 14, 1818.
(To Mr. H. Pago.)

"DEAR FRIEND,—Am I one of the happy number who can find rest in Jesus' arms? No. This blessing is too great for such a wretch as I. I can have no rest. My way is dark, and leads to hell; I know I deserve hell. Can there be any mercy in Christ for such a sinner as I am? O my sins! my sins! How many thousands and thousands of times have I sinned against that just and holy God! I have been crucifying the Savior afresh, and still go on adding sin to sin. What an awful condition I am in. If I stay here, I shall perish. If I go back to the vanities of the world, I shall certainly perish. Now what shall I do?

"You say I must go to Christ; but I cannot go to him. What shall I do to go to him? I must do something before I can go to him. I cannot go to him with such a wicked heart, and such a hard one. 'A broken and contrite heart he will not despise;' but my heart is hard as a stone, and I cannot do any thing to better it; for the more I do, the worse I am. I would, but can't repent. Though I endeavor oft, this stony heart can never relent till Jesus makes it soft. I feel stupid, dead and cold. I cannot see half enough of myself; I want to see the very worst of my heart. The Bible tells me, if I will confess my sins and forsake them, I shall find mercy; but I do not as I ought, for I can do nothing without a higher power than mine.

"Please to write again, and believe me your poor sinful and perishing friend,

"A—— W——"

To this letter he wrote the following answer:

"Coventry, March 21, 1818.
(To Miss A—— W——.)

"True, as you say, you are in an awful condition. Christ calls you by his Spirit to come to him as a weary and heavy laden sinner, that he may give you rest; but your own heart opposes him, and Satan would lead you to despair. Thus the great conflict bows you down, and you are ready to die.

"You say your heart is so hard that you cannot go to Christ. O! go to him, and he will break it. Go to him with all your pollution; for you will attempt in vain to make your heart better by your own exertions. Cry to Jesus to break this heart of stone and give you a heart of flesh. Pour out your whole soul to him. Take all your burden of sins and leave them at his cross. His blood shall cleanse them all away. Every thing that keeps you back from Christ is a sin that needs to be repented of.

"You say you cannot repent. Can you not hate sin, which has caused you so much sorrow—loath, abhor it, and turn from it? I beseech you grieve not the Spirit by finding fault with God. The guilt and the sin are all your own. How long has God spared you while rejecting the offers of his mercy! Those offers still press upon your heart. If you continue to reject them, it is at the peril of your soul. Accept them, I entreat you. There is no other way whereby you can be saved.

"Your sincere friend,

"H. PAGE"

On May 13, 1818, we find the following memorandum, embracing a resolution, the spirit of which appears habitually to have influenced his mind; and doubtless constituted, under God, the main spring of his fidelity and the ground of his success.

"I have lately had sweet communion with some of my fellow Christians, while we each related our particular feelings and exercises. What a happy result would follow, were we always, at every opportunity, to make religion our theme; and not merely talk of it in general, but come home to our own souls, and unbosom our feelings to each other—our doubts and joys, and fears, and woes. I have lately formed a resolution, which I pray God to assist me to perform:

"RESOLVED, *whenever possible, to address my brethren and sisters on the concerns of eternity, and endeavor to stir up both them and myself to diligence and engagedness in the great work of saving souls.*

"Happy news, that any of the dear pupils of my school the last winter are brought to see themselves undone sinners. The Lord grant that the time may be near, when this may be true of every dear youth and child among us. May none turn back, but all resolve to find salvation, or perish pleading for mercy."

"Coventry, June 16, 1818.
(To Rev. E. T. W——, his late Pastor.)

"RESPECTED AND DEAR SIR,—Can you believe that God is in the midst of us? Praised be his name, that his mercy is not clean gone for ever. Some of our youth appear to be under the strivings of the Spirit. I have conversed with *five* whose tears bore witness that they were not wholly secure. God only knows what will be the result; but it is fully impressed on my mind, that, could I see Christians generally earnest at the throne of grace, and engaged in the work, we should witness a precious ingathering of souls. Do pray for us, that the cloud which seems to be hovering over us, may not pass away till it shall pour down a refreshing shower upon this people.

"A few months since, I almost felt that I had no more opportunity for usefulness here; but now *I see a wide field open before me even in the midst of us.* Every day presents its calls to be at work for the Lord.

"O for a watchman to stand on these walls; to repair their breaches; and to guide the inquiring sinner to Christ, and the humble penitent in the way of peace."

At the same date he writes to another: "I have undertaken rather a hard task; but trust the Lord will in due time accomplish it. It is to *endeavor to stir up my brethren and sisters in the church to be earnest for a revival of religion.* I find in all an acknowledged neglect of duty; and in some it is mourned over apparently with a godly sorrow. I do hope for better times. I have felt an assurance that God was about to visit us in mercy."

It was probably not far from this time, that he prepared the following cards, and had them printed in a cheap form for distribution.

———

"REMEMBER, FELLOW MORTAL, YOU ARE BOUND TO ETERNITY! Death will soon overtake you. Heaven and hell are before you. Awake, if you would escape the torments of despair! Awake, and make your peace with God."

"MORTAL, CONSIDER!

"You are on the borders of *eternity*. Heaven with all its glories, or hell with all its horrors, is before you. If you are yet unreconciled to God, I entreat you this day to repent and believe on the Lord Jesus Christ—tomorrow you may be writhing in the torments of the damned! Haste, haste to him, and he will have mercy upon you, and save your soul from eternal death."

"PRISONER OF HOPE,

"Behold, He who has the keys of death and hell proclaims liberty to the captives, and the opening of the prison doors to them that are bound! Listen to the sweet notes of deliverance. Shake off the galling chains of sin by repentance and faith in the Lord Jesus Christ, and lay hold on the hope set before you. Escape, escape, while the door of mercy is open—escape, before you are thrust into the inner prison of everlasting despair."

"TODAY,

"If you will hear the voice of God, O fellow-sinner, harden not your heart. This night, should you lie down careless in sin, you may awake in an eternal hell. Escape for your life. Delay not. 'Now is the accepted time: behold, now is the day of salvation!'"

"FELLOW CHRISTIAN,

"Is it not high time to awake out of sleep? How many of your acquaintance and dear friends are on the broad road to death? Can you bear to see them hastening down to hell, and not cry unto God to have mercy on them, and pluck them as brands from the burning? O, my friend, the time is short. What we do must be done quickly. Death stands at the door; and how dreadful our surprise, if, when he enters, we be found sleeping!"

"Sabbath, July 5, 1818.

(To Miss C—— R——, one of his late pupils.)

"How is it now with your immortal soul? Are you yet at enmity with God? I have long wished for an opportunity to make these inquiries, and entreat you to flee from the wrath to come; but since our school closed, this has been denied me. And now, in view of your awful danger, and in love to your soul, permit me once more to press upon you the necessity of speedy repentance.

"O Caroline, while out of Christ, how dreadful is your condition!

No ray of hope remains for you, if you live and die in this state; but you must for ever lie down in the torments of the damned—for ever dwell with devouring fire!

"Will you go on neglecting this precious season, when the Holy Spirit is striving among us? Can you rest secure, while your acquaintance and friends are anxiously inquiring what they must do to be saved? O, my friend, consider how brief is your life. Death lies in ambush; suddenly the fatal dart may be hurled; and if Christ is not yours, your soul will be lost.

"This may be the Spirit's last call. If you now reject him, he may return to you no more for ever. Will you not take up in earnest the great subject of the salvation of your own soul, feel your guilt and your danger, and fly to the arms of the blessed Savior? 'Now is the accepted time—now is the day of salvation.' Rest not one moment till you have secured the pearl of great price. Sleep not in sin, lest you awake in an eternal hell; where 'the smoke of their torment ascendeth up for ever and ever.' O Caroline, repent now, and believe in the Lord Jesus Christ, and you shall be saved.

"With earnest prayers for you, your friend,

"H. PAGE"

"*Friday, P. M. July* 24, 1818.

(To Miss E—— H—— R——.)

"MY DEAR FRIEND,—At your request, I with pleasure improve a few moments in writing on the concerns of the soul. I have trembled, and still tremble for you and others. Can it be possible, O Eliza, can it be possible, that any, whose attention has been awakened, are becoming insensible of their danger? Can any be so unwise as not to cherish the influences of the Spirit while he calls them to repent and fly to that refuge, out of which God has declared himself 'a consuming fire?' Can any be discouraged, while the joys of heaven and the woes of the damned are at stake?

"Remember, for your consolation, that 'the kingdom of heaven suffereth violence, and the violent take it by force.' Go then to the throne of grace, and resolve, with Jacob of old, 'I will not let thee go, except thou bless me.' Every delay is fraught with imminent danger. Every moment you neglect coming to Christ your sins are increasing. Will you not now cease your opposition, and this night go and throw yourself unreservedly on the mercy of Christ? Mercy calls. Mercy entreats. O Eliza, go now to Christ, and let mercy save you. Don't depend on what you do. It will be altogether in vain. Your best services need pardon through atoning blood. Put on the white robe of Christ's righteousness, and you shall be happy. I entreat you, my dear friend, press on—press on.

"In great haste, your affectionate friend,   H. PAGE"

"Coventry, August 7, 1818.
(To S—— K——.)

"Can you yet calmly submit yourself to Christ? Have you been to him with all your pollution upon you, crying, 'Here am I, a poor undone sinner, wholly unworthy of thy favor, justly condemned to eternal death; take me as I am; Lord, save me, or I perish?' Can you now, by faith, embrace him as your Savior? Is it your earnest desire to do all in your power to advance his cause and glory? Can you renounce every worldly object for Christ? If so, happy are you. But if not, your case is dreadful indeed. Faithfully examine yourself by the word of God, and rest not one moment till you have evidence that you have chosen that good part which can never be taken from you. Be faithful, O be faithful unto death. Let nothing turn you from seeking and serving the Lord.

"Your affectionate friend,

"H. Page"

The following is one of the requests for his counsel and prayers, which he frequently received:

"Mr. Page,—I need your kind instructions now more than ever. I feel willing to renounce every worldly object for Christ. O what is this world! Time is short, eternity is long. I know what I must do; but I find a dreadful, stubborn heart. Do advise me. How shall I get to Christ? I seek for happiness, but find none. I fear my companions are growing indifferent about their future state. S—— gets no relief. Do remember us in your prayers.

"E. H. R."

The following was our brother's reply to this affecting letter:

"Friday, P. M. Sept. 12, 1818.

"Friend E——, Do you really 'feel willing to renounce every worldly object for Christ?' If this is so, you can unreservedly give up all confidence in your own doings or righteousness, all love of sin; and Christ has indeed found the chief place in your heart. But beware of a false hope; you had better spend all your days in despondence, than find at last that you were self-deceived.

"You speak of a stubborn heart. Ah, E——, I know what you mean. This heart has felt that dreadful opposition to our dear Redeemer, who gave himself to be crucified that we might live. How ungrateful! How astonishing, that such love should be requited thus! My friend, how can you help loving him, who has done so much for you? How can you help giving your heart to him, who invites you in such sweet accents of mercy?

"You ask, 'How shall I go to Christ?' Go just as you are, with no delay to make yourself better. Go humble, penitent, believing. Go to him as your *only refuge*, (for you have found all others fail,) and be assured he will receive you. You will go. It seems to me you cannot help it. My poor prayers are poured out to God for you.

"With sincere affection,

"H. PAGE"

To a cousin in P——, N. Y. he wrote respecting their friends and the state of religion, mentioning that the church had observed a day of fasting and prayer for the outpouring of the Spirit; and then proceeds in endeavors to do good to the person addressed, to his family, and those around him:

"You have not yet, it seems, taken hold of the promises of the Gospel; not yet laid down the weapons of your rebellion. But will you not submit to Christ? O, consider his agony in the garden and on the cross—and for whom was all this? It was, dear Sir, for you, if you will not reject his bleeding love; for you, his sweat was as it were blood; for you, he was scourged and buffeted; for you, he ascended the hill of Calvary; for you, he was nailed to the cross; for you, he was forsaken of God; for you, he yielded up the ghost.

"Now, can you say you will not accept the salvation purchased by such sufferings? Will you disregard the invitations and entreaties of this bleeding Savior, and go on crucifying him afresh! O you will not, you cannot despise and reject such love—you will not be guilty of such black ingratitude.

"If you have not already done it, I beseech you go now to Jesus as a heavy laden sinner; go as a self condemned criminal; offer yourself to him, a living sacrifice; and find rest to your soul.

"Does your companion, my dear cousin, know by sweet experience how precious is the Savior's love? She has been brought to the borders of the grave. Was it indeed dark; or did the Son of God enlighten the prospect, and stand as her conductor to eternal glory? My dear cousin, let it not be in vain that you are spared. Be wise for eternity. Make the Savior your friend and portion.

"Will Christians around you make this world their God, and do nothing for the salvation of perishing sinners? How is it possible that any who have tasted the love of God can rest, while on every side sinners are thoughtlessly going down to hell? Christians in P—— must awake. Their work is great, and their time is short. While they are sleeping in neglect of effectual fervent prayer, they are, by their neglect, peopling the world of perdition. But though Christians sleep, sinners have no excuse. They know their Master's will, and do it not.

"How is it with Joseph and Daniel? Are they yet in the ark of safety?

Tell them the floods of Divine wrath are fast accumulating, and unless they repent they must likewise perish.

"Your affectionate friend and cousin,

"H. PAGE"

In replying to this letter some months after, his cousin says: "When your letter was received, it was a dagger to my soul; but now, my dear cousin, *I think I know something by experience of the excellency of religion,* and the peace there is in casting all my burdens on him who cares for us. Within a few weeks, I have taken real satisfaction in reading that kind letter. I thank you for it. Do now write me again."

CHAPTER 3

RESIDENCE OF TWO MONTHS IN BOSTON, AND NEARLY
THREE YEARS IN COVENTRY.

The shock which the constitution of Mr. Page received in his severe illness in 1814, partially disabled him from pursuing the more laborious
mechanical employments; and in October, 1818, he visited Boston, and
spent a few weeks in writing up the books of a mercantile house, hoping
to see some opening in which he might engage in engraving, to which he
seems to have had a native predilection, or in teaching. His letters to his
family serve to show how his Christian character was developed in the new
circumstances in which he was then placed, in the heart of a bustling city.

"*Boston, Saturday evening, Oct.* 17, 1818.
(To Mrs. Page.)

"I have had occasion to sympathize this evening with my hostess, a
widow whose *only son has this day sailed for Brazil.* A few days since, he
said to his mother: 'There is my Bible, I must take that.' I gave him a few
Tracts, with which he was much gratified. His mother has scarcely tasted
food today. Her life has been a series of trouble; but I fear it has not all
brought her to Christ. I also gave a few Tracts to the captain of a vessel sail-
ing for Africa, who thinks them very useful among seamen.

"You can have no idea of the *wickedness which prevails here.* Though
much is doing for the cause of Zion, thousands in Boston live like the heathen, profaning and blaspheming the name of God. When I look around
and see so many souls hastening to destruction, I am led to inquire, Is there
no help? Will not Christians awake? and will not the Lord come down with
his mighty power and shake the multitude of evil doers?

"Last Sabbath morning heard Rev. Mr. D——, from 'Let me die the
death of the righteous,' etc. His object was to prove that impenitent sinners
do not really wish the pure joys and employments of heaven, which he did

most clearly. Dined with Mr. D—— H——, and then accompanied him to *the Sabbath School;* and it was a most interesting and animating spectacle. This was the first Sabbath School established in Boston, and contains about 70 or 75 scholars. It was opened with prayer by the superintendent, and then the recitations began. Three of the scholars recited Scripture to me, two of whom had committed to memory about 120 verses each, since the last Sabbath. I took the opportunity to speak to them on the concerns of their souls, directing my conversation to one at first, but the others immediately crowded up as if eager to hear. The school is closed with singing, when the scholars accompany their instructors to church. Tomorrow I expect to visit the school again, *and learn more of the methods of proceeding."*

After describing various meetings which he attended during the week, he thus proceeds:

"Is there no more prospect of an awakening in Coventry? Will sinners—can they continue to rush headlong to ruin? Will the church still sleep? How astonishing! Shall we who love Christ be unconcerned for our fellow-beings who are hastening to despair? I wish to see S—— and E——, (to whom he had written as above,) to tell them again to repent and believe in Jesus.

"*Sabbath evening.* This morning I attended Rev. Mr. Paul's meeting, and heard a colored preacher from the words, 'If we sin, we have an Advocate,' etc. Thence again to the Sabbath School, where I found the male and female schools assembled in one room. Upwards of two hundred children were present, and many of their parents who had been invited to attend. After prayer, animating addresses were delivered to the parents and children. Some of the parents were in tears.

"In the afternoon, heard a very solemn discourse from the words, 'What must I do to be saved?' The *singing* was excellent. You know English and other scientific music is condemned as being too slow, and wanting life. This may be true as it is sometimes performed; but as sung here, it is full of spirit. The words are spoken distinctly, and there is far more animation and expression than we usually hear.

"I meet with some trials here, which I hope will be for my good. Two *Universalist ministers* are dragging many, I fear, with themselves down to hell. Do let us, my dear wife, be doing. Life will soon close; and O the condemnation of being found unprofitable servants. Do not delay to write.

"With many prayers for yourself and the babes,

"H. PAGE"

"Boston, Sabbath evening, Nov. 1, 1818.
(To the same.)

"Last Sabbath morning I heard the Rev. Dr. Worcester, of Salem; and in the afternoon, Rev. Mr. J——, at the Seaman's church. In the evening attended a prayer-meeting consisting chiefly of sailors, and at the close *conversed freely with several,* who begged me to come again.

"During the day *I met a sailor on the wharf,* who told me he had been a prisoner at Newfoundland, and was put upon trial; but nothing was found against him, and he was liberated. I told him we must meet another and more solemn trial in the day of judgment, when, without an interest in Christ, we must be condemned eternally. He was silent. I entreated him to think of these things, and be prepared; for they were near at hand.

"This morning and afternoon I have heard the Rev. Levi Parsons, who is going on a mission to Jerusalem. He appears much engaged for the salvation of souls, and preaches faithfully the terrors of the Lord. What an interesting field is this for the man of God! May the smiles of heaven attend him and his companion in labors, who are to be ordained the present week. May they be made instruments of renewing the pure worship of that Savior who there suffered for man's redemption.

"*Monday evening,* 9 *o'clock.* Just returned from the *monthly concert,* and have been richly entertained. Mr. Evarts communicated a great deal of interesting intelligence, chiefly respecting the missions among the Cherokees and Choctaws. Your heart would have been made joyful in hearing it. Many very encouraging and interesting incidents were mentioned. At the close, a contribution was taken up for the mission at Jerusalem."

"Boston, Nov. 7, 1818.
(To the same.)

"When I read your remark, that God has evidently a controversy with the church in Coventry, my tears involuntarily flowed. O how dreadful, that a church should hinder the salvation of souls! And those dear ones who have long been inquiring—how affecting to consider that hardly any, even of professed Christians, seem to care whether they go to destruction or not! And can this be so? Alas! what reason have we to think otherwise?

"I have just passed through *a most affecting scene.* On last Sabbath evening I went alone to the house where I had attended a prayer-meeting a week previous; but found there was no meeting, and that, under the same roof, a man was very sick. His wife, who is pious, appeared grateful for my call, gave me an account of their circumstances, and informed me that her husband had been a professed Universalist; but of late she thought his confidence in that error was shaken; though he would frequently argue the subject with her and others, even on his sick, and, she feared, his dying bed. She informed him I was present, and asked if he wished prayer. He said he did. I told him I would comply—remarking that, as he seemed near to death, he must probably soon meet the eternal God, and asking if he felt prepared. He intimated that he did.

"'Do you think you have experienced that change of heart which is spoken of in the word of God as essential to salvation?'

"'Have I repented of my sins,' (said he to himself,) 'and believed on the Lord Jesus Christ?'

"'Do you love Christ?' said I. 'Is he the one altogether lovely?'

"'Yes, he is lovely to me. I hope to be saved by him.'

"'Do you believe all will be saved by Christ?'

"'Yes, I think so.'

"'What do you think of the passage, These shall go away into everlasting punishment?'

"'I cannot tell what it means.'

"'We read also, The wicked shall be turned into hell, and all the nations that forget God.'

"'Then,' said he, 'I must go there.'

"He seemed somewhat exhausted, and I was about to close my interview, when he again asked me to pray with him.

"'What petition shall I offer?' said I. 'Shall I ask that your heart may be changed?'

"'Yes,' said he, 'and that I may be purified.'

"Neighbors in the house were called in, and prayer was made in his behalf, amidst sobs and tears. His wife begged me to call again, which I did, with Mr. D. a young clergyman. He was evidently declining, but gave us no more satisfaction respecting his state.

"After we left him, he had much conversation with Rev. Mr. J——, and expressed his conviction of his ruin by sin; his renunciation of all the former grounds of his hope; his reliance solely upon Christ, and his peace and joy in him. He died the following day. His wife had long prayed earnestly for his conversion; and at last, when she had almost given him up as lost, had the satisfaction of seeing him give such evidence as he could in his last hours, that he fell asleep in Jesus."

His next letter is dated at *Coventry, Feb.* 13, 1819, and expresses his joy, that, on the 10th of the following month, the Rev. G. A. C—— was to be ordained as pastor.

"*Saturday evening.*—This day I have endeavored to observe as a day of humiliation, fasting, and prayer for the outpouring of the Spirit. I find so much in me that is unhumbled, that I have reason to fear the day has been spent in vain. Several now appear anxious for their souls. God grant that they may be brought to bow submissive at the feet of Jesus, and that the hearts of Christians may be prepared for the special presence of God among us. O what shall be done in this stubborn, unyielding frame of mind!"

Within the progress of a few weeks his heart was cheered and refreshed by a visit, with his beloved pastor, to a church some miles distant, which was enjoying a precious revival of religion.

"As I entered the sanctuary, (he says,) joy beamed in the countenances of numbers, while others seemed borne down with a heavy load. Solemn silence reigned, interrupted only by occasional sighs and tears. Every eye was fixed, and every ear listening as to a message from the Lord. When the service closed, several remained to converse on the subject of their salvation.

"They dispersed for a little time; and at sunset the youth were seen assembling in groups, till the room was filled with near 200 immortal beings. All was silent as the house of death. The most profound attention evinced that the Lord was there. When the exercises were closed, and the blessing pronounced, not one moved to leave the house. All stood and seemed to say, 'We *cannot* go. Tell us more of Christ, and how to gain an interest in his atoning blood.'

"After a few moments, the minister, who had addressed them, began to converse with an individual near him; but all seemed eager to press forward, that they might hear for their own benefit. None appeared indifferent. Solemnity, sorrow, or joy was depicted in every countenance. The audience were seated, and nearly all in the house were addressed individually in reference to their own personal salvation. None wished to avoid being questioned, or being warned that, unless they repented of their sins and fled to Christ by a living faith, they must be lost."

This account Mr. Page embodied in an anonymous paper sent in with others to be read in the "Biblical School," in Coventry, in which a large number of youth united for the study of the Bible, and mutual, intellectual, moral and religious improvement.

"Our minister (he adds) has seen among another people anxious souls flocking to Christ. What must have been his reflections, surrounded by such a crowd of inquirers, as he turned his thoughts to his own flock—his church cold and languid—the youth thoughtless and gay, pressing on their way to eternal despair! How must his heart have sunk within him!

"And shall he find no inquiring souls here? Shall his heart *never* be gladdened by hearing the earnest inquiry, 'What must we do to be saved?' Shall we suffer *him* to go mourning all the day over so many hurrying to perdition? Shall we suffer *ourselves* to be lulled in security, and thus be eternally ruined? O it is time, it is high time to awake."

Having received a fresh supply of Tracts, he immediately enclosed two of them to impenitent friends in notes, of which the following is one:

"June 22, 1819.
(To L. S.)

"DEAR BROTHER,—Will you and your companion oblige me so much as to give the enclosed an attentive perusal before you go to rest this night? I have just received it, and feel peculiarly anxious that you should prayerfully consider the all-important subject it presents.

"With earnest solicitude for your eternal welfare, I am your brother,

"H. PAGE"

The season of God's mercy was indeed at hand. On the 20th of June he thus wrote to Mrs. W——:

"MY DEAR FRIEND,—I have delayed till I can do it no longer. I know the joy you will feel at the repentance of sinners in Coventry. When I wrote you last, all was gloomy, except the prospect that God was about to place over us a spiritual guide. He has been indefatigable. For a time all *applauded*, but none seemed to be *moved*.

"A meeting of the church was called, when all the male members were questioned with regard to their feelings. All confessed criminal coldness and want of spiritual life. The question was then put, 'Are we not called to make some special exertions that the work of God may be revived?' This was acknowledged, and it was agreed to hold prayer meetings in different neighborhoods.

"Two weeks after, another meeting was called, which 'all who felt anxious for a revival of religion were invited to attend.' This led to self-examination. 'Shall I go?' was the language of many. 'I cannot say I am one of those invited, but I dare not stay away.' Members of the church and others attended, and the meeting was full. The time was spent in exhortation and prayer, and some signs of life appeared.

"The next week a similar meeting was held, when every one who chose it was conversed with individually, and it appeared that some were inquiring. A work of grace was then progressing in B——, and had now entered our borders.

"A few of the church appear to be engaged. They found that they had wandered far, very far from God. Conversation meetings for inquirers are held weekly. Mr. and Mrs. G—— are now rejoicing in the Lord. Mrs. R——, Miss M—— W——, and Miss J—— are indulging a hope. The progress of the work has seemed to be exactly in accordance with the spirituality, the prayers and exertions of Christians. Sometimes the prospect looks dark, but at others more encouraging. It is the Lord's work, and he alone can carry it on. The hopes of many professors of religion are shaken. Our minister has repeatedly told us, that if we cannot be engaged in such a time as this, we had better conclude that we are not Christians.

"Yesterday Rev. Mr. N—— preached twice in different neighborhoods. I could say a great deal, but must not add.

"With Christian affection, your friend,

"H. PAGE"

Under date of July 9, in a hasty note to a friend, he says: "We have such a season here as we never had before: the Lord is doing wonders, and we hope and believe he is about to work still greater. Could you see the change wrought in S——, (referred to December, 1815, and June, 1819,) you would be delighted. He seems indeed like one new born, through the energies of the Holy Ghost."

Mr. Page always regarded a season of the outpouring of the Holy Spirit as *the harvest time of souls;* and it is hard to say whether his holy joy in God, his amazing sense of responsibility, his importunate prayers, or incessant efforts, most abounded. He seems to have been so intently engaged in promoting the work, that he made only a few brief notices of what was passing, with his pen. Among these is a list of *seventy-nine* individuals who in that revival obtained hope in Christ; *sixty-six* of whom were added to the church.

On the 9th of August he thus addressed a young woman, whose case he seems to have considered almost hopeless:

"An affectionate regard for your immortal interests has induced me to write a few lines, though I know not that they will be welcome or beneficial. While others have been accepting Christ, I have anxiously hoped to hear the same of you. Shall no Christian's heart be cheered by such intelligence? Shall neither man nor God hear from your lips: 'O my sins, my sins, I fear they will ruin my soul for ever?' Shall no prayer, 'God be merciful to me a sinner,' break from your heart?

"I know you would not dare make light of the influences of the Holy Spirit; and is there not evidence sufficient to convince the most obstinate that the Lord is indeed among us? Who then will be on the Lord's side? Will you not come as a humble penitent, and cast yourself at his feet? Will you not now, by faith in Christ, become a friend of God, and an heir of glory?

"May I not hope that you are now determined to break your league with sin and the enemy of souls, before the impending storm of God's wrath shall fall upon you, when the only answer to your despairing cry shall be, FOR EVER—FOR EVER—FOR EVER! O do not let a deceitful heart beguile you. You have a soul at stake worth millions of worlds, and which must live eternally in the joys of heaven or the agonies of hell. On no other subject should I address you, but on the momentous concerns of the soul you will not feel that I need apologize for the performance of duty.

"With esteem, your friend,

"H. PAGE"

In a letter, September 20, he says: "It is uncertain whether I go to Boston this fall. *I cannot leave this interesting field of exertion and scene of wonders.*"

A subsequent letter, chiefly occupied with statements respecting the revival, contains the following paragraph:

"In the midst of mercy, God has recently reminded us, by a most afflictive providence, that youth is with many the only time for securing the salvation of the soul. O—— P——, aged twenty-two, about two weeks since was called into eternity. But he died in faith, as we trust. He was hopefully converted the summer past, *just in time to escape the wrath to come.*"

To a communication from S—— L——, expressing renewed anxiety for himself as a sinner, and requesting Mr. Page's prayers and counsel, he thus replied:

"*Coventry,* 11*th* Dec. 1819.

"MY DEAR SIR,—It is with peculiar satisfaction that I improve the opportunity you have given me to address you on the momentous interests of your own soul. You have frankly disclosed your feelings, and I am unusually anxious that you should cast your burdens on the Lord, and give him your whole heart. You are now at an awful *crisis.* Your eternal all may depend on the course you take. The Lord has taught you by his Spirit, that you are a wretched, perishing sinner. You feel that you have no preparation for heaven, and see nothing before you but eternal wo. O my friend, *there is a refuge.* The Lord Jesus invites, in melting strains, 'Look to me, and live. Come unto me, and find rest.' O, go to him *now,* as you value your precious, immortal soul.

"But you ask, 'How shall I go to him with this hard impenitent heart?' Christ, my friend, is ready to soften and sanctify it by his own blood. Go to him *just as you are*—poor—needy—empty—wretched—only *go to him.* His grace is free. It will be his joy now to receive you. And will you not go? O make now one determined effort in the strength of God. Break through all opposition from within and from without. Cast yourself at the feet of Jesus, and cry, 'Lord, save me, or I perish.'

"Your dear friend went to Christ, and is now, we trust, in heaven.

Follow his example in loving the Savior, and you may follow him to glory. Death to him was welcome, so it may be to you. There was a fullness in Christ for him, so there is for you. The blessed fountain is set open, and *whosoever will* may 'take of the waters of life freely.'

"May I not indulge the hope and expectation, that, before you shall lay down this sheet, you will have made the successful resolve, and fled for refuge to the ark of safety; and that, when next we meet, you will tell me what glorious things God has done for your soul? O my friend, God has said his Spirit shall not always strive. I fear, should you delay a little longer, he will depart from you, never to return.

"With earnest prayer for you, your affectionate friend,

"H. PAGE"

"*Coventry, Friday evening, Dec.* 24, 1819.
(To Miss J—— A—— L——.)

"I am very anxious to know how you are now. Are you yet rejoicing in hope; or have you turned again to the follies of this flattering and deceitful world? O my friend, I long to hear from you. I long to hear that you have chosen that good part which shall never be taken away. Have you, do tell me, have you forgotten our last interview? Have you performed the sacred promise to give yourself and your all to Christ? Have you submitted to his will, and determined to die a beggar at his feet? Do write me immediately. I wait, impatient to hear. Resist temptation. Quench not the Spirit. Pray without ceasing. Repent and believe in the Lord Jesus Christ, and you shall be saved.

"I am now keeping school—*some encouraging prospects among my scholars*. Friends feel anxious for you. I can assure you, you have many fervent petitions ascending from the heart to God in your behalf.

"With much affection, your friend and cousin,

"H. PAGE"

Of his efforts for the eternal welfare of the pupils of his school, a Christian friend says, in a letter written since his death, "a number of ladies, who, when in youth, attended this school, still feel under great obligations to him and to God for *his faithful and untiring efforts* for their salvation, and *attribute their conversion, under God, to his instrumentality.*"

So much was his mind engrossed with the subject of the salvation of the young, that in January he prepared an article, in which were clustered some of the MOTIVES TO EARLY PIETY; which, in the hope that it would meet the eye of those under his care, and others, he sent for insertion in the Guardian, a small and useful monthly periodical. We retain enough of the article to show what place this subject held in the mind and heart of the writer.

"My dear young Friend,—While I see so many youth hastening unprepared to eternity, I cannot forbear calling to you to stop for a moment, and consider what affecting motives urge you to make your peace with God.

"Your *Christian friends* earnestly desire your salvation. They see your danger. They know that, unless your heart is renewed by the Holy Spirit, your soul must be lost. They plead with you. They weep and pray for you night and day. They long to rejoice over you as a new-born heir of heaven.

"The *angels of God* desire your salvation. Yes, their golden harps are tuned to raise a louder song of joy over every one who will repent. Will you not be the first to cause the arches of heaven to re-echo, that another wanderer has returned? Shall angels long for your salvation, and you be unconcerned about it yourself? But more,

"*Christ himself* desires your salvation. For this he became 'a man of sorrows and acquainted with grief.' For this he endured the agony of the garden and the cross. He calls you, by his word, by his providence, and by his Spirit. He declares that he 'is not willing that any should perish, but that all should come to repentance.' And shall he call in vain? Is it nothing to you, that he shed his precious blood, and bore the wrath of Jehovah for perishing sinners? O heart of adamant, that will not melt in view of such condescension, suffering, and love! O vile ingratitude, that can behold, unmoved, the 'Son of God in tears,' offering himself for man's redemption!

"Consider also *the glories of heaven*. There is the throne of God and of the Lamb. There, the pure river of the water of life for ever flows. There, saints and angels offer their unceasing praises. There, your departed Christian friends mingle their voices with the heavenly choir. There, all unite in shouting 'Alleluia, Alleluia, for the Lord God omnipotent reigneth,' 'Blessing, and honor, and glory, and power be unto him that sitteth on the throne, and unto the Lamb for ever and ever.' There, every humble penitent at last arrives. There, is the consummation of all his happiness.

"Think too of *the misery of hell*. O the horrors of despair! What pencil can paint, or what pen describe them! Weeping, and wailing, and gnashing of teeth constitute the horrid discord of the abodes of the damned. There the stings of a guilty conscience, that worm that never dies; heart-rending reflections on murdered time; the view of saints in glory afar off; the surrounding gloom of the infernal pit; unavailing lamentations and despair, all conspire to render their misery complete. O, 'who can dwell with devouring fire? Who can inhabit everlasting burnings?'

"Consider *the worth of the soul.* Its value can be measured only by eternity. When millions of millions of ages shall have rolled away, your soul will still be active, and its capacity to suffer or enjoy for ever increasing.

"*Death is rapidly approaching.* Perhaps this night you will close your eyes to wake in eternity. Thousands have been thus surprised. How many of your companions are gone, never to return! Their state is fixed. They are now enduring the wrath of God, or singing his praises in the paradise above. Whoever you are, you may be assured that death is nigh to you. To him you must yield, willing or unwilling; and eternal wo must be your doom, unless you haste to Christ, the only refuge from the impending storm.

"*The day of judgment* is at hand. Soon the loud trump of the archangel will awake the sleeping dead; and you among them will come forth to 'the resurrection of life,' or 'the resurrection of damnation.' Then the Savior, whom you have loved, or despised, will appear in the clouds of heaven, to give to every one 'according as his work shall be.' Before him you must stand with assembled millions, while he bids you depart, or welcomes you to a seat at his right hand.

"Other motives might be urged, but if these will not awaken you to a sense of your danger, others would be unavailing. Now you have a day of grace. Now the saints are praying for you; the angels of God wait to rejoice over you; the Lord Jesus Christ, by his word and by his Spirit, is entreating you to come; the glories of heaven are offered you; the miseries of hell are unveiled to your view; while the worth of your soul, the rapid approach of death and judgment, urge you to make haste—to escape for your life from the destruction that awaits you. O my young friend, as you value your eternal wellbeing, I beseech you awake from this slumber. Arise and go to Jesus. Go to him a humble beggar; go penitent and believing. None such were ever sent empty away. While you tarry, your sins are accumulating, your danger is increasing. Delay a little longer, and your soul, your precious, immortal soul, is lost for ever."

"*Coventry, after school, Friday, March* 10, 1820.
(To Miss J—— A—— L——.)

"Your letter gave me peculiar pleasure, as it contained expressions of a hope that you have passed from death unto life. Yet when we consider the deceitfulness of the heart, and the temptations of the adversary, it becomes us to rejoice with trembling. Is Christ indeed precious to you? O happy soul! Happy even in the midst of adversity; happy in life, happy in death, and happy for ever. I long to know more particularly what is your state, and what have been your exercises, both before and since your conversion. Let me entreat you to be faithful to your own soul and to God. Seek also *the eternal welfare of your companions.* You know not how much you may yet do, which God shall make the means of saving souls.

"Your friend,

"H. PAGE"

"*Wednesday evening, April 4.*—This day has been observed as a day of fasting, humiliation and prayer, and has been a solemn and interesting season. Several clergymen of the vicinity were with us; having commenced visiting the churches in succession. Each minister present prayed, and addressed the crowded assembly; and the members of the church expressed, by rising, their solemn determination to be faithful, and live more in accordance with their profession. It is supposed that *about half of the towns in this state are now visited with a special out-pouring of the Holy Spirit.* We cannot but hope that God will also appear for us in mercy, though I do not know of one serious inquirer. God grant that his own people may arise to duty, the impenitent be alarmed, and that there may be a rich ingathering of souls."

On the 16th he addressed a young friend, to whom, it appears he had agreed to write, first on the subject of education and mental improvement, and then on "the '*one thing needful,*' without which all other acquisitions are vain"—requesting in return "a free expression of opinions and feeling *on both subjects.*" In the reply, the former subject seems to be wholly overlooked.

"The deep interest which you have manifested for my immortal soul," says the writer, "I can never, no, never forget. I have thought much on the contents of your letter. I am deeply sensible that religion alone is worth living for. You will probably say, 'then why not embrace it?' I can only reply that it is owing entirely to the wickedness of my heart, which has long been pursuing the pleasures of the world. If I perish, I know I have nothing to plead in excuse for rejecting the offers of mercy. I feel in need of your advice, and beg you not to forget me when interceding at the throne of grace.

"Yours respectfully,

"C—— H—— H——"

On the 16th April he commenced a correspondence with A. K., a beloved relative now in the ministry, for their mutual benefit in reference both to the present and a future life. In this letter he says:

"You complain of insensibility to the great concerns of eternity; and, my friend, you are not alone in this. I know of no better way to be delivered from it, than to GO FORWARD *in every known duty, relying on the aids of the Holy Spirit.* It appears that this is the best means of promoting a revival of religion in our own hearts, and of being useful to others. Let us, dear brother, be more active. How many of our acquaintance, over whom we may perhaps have influence, *have we left* without faithfully performing our duty to their souls! We know that without religion they are lost. Let us then act accordingly."

One expression in the above clearly implies, that, faithful as he had been, there was present before his mind, not the many he had warned, but *the great number remaining*, for whose salvation he had individually done nothing effectual.

The following attempt to reach the heart of a young man whom he highly esteemed, but who was only 'almost persuaded to be a Christian,' affords another illustration of the manner in which he carried out his desires and purposes to do good.

> "*Coventry, Friday evening, April* 20, 1821.
> (To Mr. C. P.)

"MY DEAR FRIEND—I think I feel more and more interested in your welfare, and anxious that you may be useful, especially in promoting the salvation of men. But without the hope that you are yourself interested in the Savior's love, how can you labor for the salvation of others? Were your tongue unloosed, and your heart warm with love to God and souls, how might you take your companions by the hand, and entreat them, in Christ's stead, to be reconciled to God! How would you retire to your closet and agonize in prayer in their behalf! Whenever you looked upon them, how would your heart swell within you, from a sense of their danger! How would you weep in secret places over their impenitence, and dreadful indifference to eternal things.

"But, alas! for this you are not prepared. No one has ever heard you entreating sinners to flee from the wrath to come—no humble prayer has ever ascended from your heart to God in their behalf. My friend, if you or I ever do any thing for God, it must be done *soon*. 'What I say unto you, I say unto all, *Watch;* for in such an hour as ye think not, the Son of man cometh.' How should I rejoice to take you by the hand as a dear brother in the Lord, and to see you far more faithful in the service of Christ than ever I have been! How happy might we be in mutual efforts here, and with what joy unite for ever in the songs of praise to redeeming love!

"That this joy may be ours, through penitence for sin, and faith in atoning blood, is the prayer of your affectionate friend,

"H. PAGE"

CHAPTER 4

RESIDENCE OF TWO MONTHS IN JEWETT CITY AND EIGHTEEN MONTHS IN COVENTRY.

Mr. Page now spent some weeks in mechanical labors in Jewett City, a manufacturing village which had recently sprung up thirty miles distant; lodging with a pious relative who there resided. His letters to his family, with a brief journal during his absence, give us additional light respecting the state of his heart, and his efforts to be useful.

"*Friday, May* 18, 1821. Left home for Jewett City. Spent the night at brother T.'s in Lebanon.—*Have had a long season of spiritual darkness,* but this evening think I enjoyed more of the light of God's countenance."

"*Saturday*, 19. Determined to endeavor to *do all my duty to all the members of brother T.'s family.* Felt a peculiar earnestness in family prayer for those who were without God. Went to the factory and *conversed with each person* employed in it, on the state of their souls. Found in them a general reluctance to come to a determination to attend immediately to the one thing needful. Two or three appeared somewhat affected in view of their state. How important, that, in conversing with the impenitent, we endeavor to *bring the truth home plainly to their hearts.* God grant that this interview may not be in vain."

It was on this or another occasion, that as he was passing a school-house in L——, he called, presented some Tracts to the teacher for her scholars, and addressed a few words to her on the subject of her own salvation; and to this brief interview she now ascribes her conversion to God.

On the same day he arrived at Jewett City; and the following letter on the evening of the succeeding day shows how soon he found something here to do for Christ.

> "*Jewett City, Sabbath evening,* 10 *o'clock.*
> (To Mrs. Page.)
> "Thus far the Lord has sustained me. I arrived here in safety last evening.

This morning heard Rev. Mr. W——, from Revelation 7:10, showing that the salvation of the sinner should all be ascribed to God. In the afternoon attended a funeral, where Mr. W. solemnly addressed a large concourse. This evening have visited at the boarding-house, where are about forty boarders. Found some there who seemed to love the cause of Christ. I remarked to Mrs. P——, that I thought we ought to have prayer meetings in the neighborhood. She gave her assent; and soon proposed that we should *commence them this evening*, and that the boarders be called in. Expecting I should be requested to lead, gave me a little heart-fluttering; but I think I had some earnestness in the performance of the duty.

"Many connected with the factory spend the Sabbath in idleness or amusement. I feel that I have here *much to do;* and O for judgment, prudence, humility, and love to God and souls, to enable me to perform it! I feel more and more the need of Divine aid, and of the prayers of others. I think my situation here will in many respects be trying. I shall need the whole armor of God. My religious privileges will be less than they have been; but it seems there is a door opening that I may be useful. *Pray for me,* my dear wife, and *engage all you can to do the same.* Give the little ones a kiss from Pa. Stay yourself on God. He knows what is for your good.

"With the tenderest affection,

"H. PAGE"

"*Monday,* 21. Proposed to one of the workmen that we hold stated prayer meetings for a revival of religion in the factory. Think we shall succeed."

"*Wednesday evening,* 22. Had a meeting of the workmen and boarders at Captain P——'s. It was agreed to hold a weekly prayer meeting on Wednesday evenings. Feel considerable anxiety for a revival of religion in the factory. There appears here a dreadful indifference to Divine things. O Lord, make the stubborn tremble, and make those whom I daily see living in sin, the trophies of thy grace!"

"*Saturday evening,* 25. Today I have heard good news from Coventry— the conversions of P. P. and J. P. For a moment I could hardly be reconciled to be away from them; but the persuasion that God has more for me to do here than there, calms my anxieties and stimulates me to act. To God I would commit my dear family. May he preserve them tonight, and give them and me a pleasant Sabbath! Today had some conversation with a universalist. Agreed with a Christian friend to make him a subject of special prayer."

"*Jewett City, Wednesday evening,* May 30.
(To Mrs. Page.)
"I received yours on Saturday, which gave me the pleasing intelligence

that P. P. and J. P. think they have found the Savior. I hope, by this time, the work has become general. It seems more and more that it was necessary for me to come away. Perhaps *I was the Achan* that prevented the blessing. It appears that God will have me remain here at present.

"On Wednesday evenings we have a prayer meeting of those connected with the factory; and a few, who love the Throne of Grace, have agreed to establish a prayer meeting on *Sabbath mornings at sunrise.* Christians here are of various religious denominations, and seem to have been discouraged. I think there are some appearances now of quickening. There appears so wide a door here for Christian effort, that I scarcely know where to begin. Several of the workmen will probably unite and take the Missionary Herald, that it may be read at the Wednesday evening meetings; but the religious state of the people, generally, is lamentable. By many the Sabbath is shamefully profaned, and the enemies of Christ seem to triumph. *I need your prayers,* and the prayers of friends, for *wisdom, grace,* and *humility.*

"Affectionately yours,

"H. Page"

The following memorandum shows briefly how he spent the next Sabbath.

"*Sabbath evening, June 3.*—This morning attended a prayer meeting at sunrise. *Seven* were present. Had a pleasant meeting. They thought they had felt for a few days a greater anxiety for a revival of religion.

"After breakfast visited Mr. F. a sick man, who has worked with us. Yesterday his case was thought to be dangerous, but today he is more comfortable. Conversed with him on the state of his soul; found him without hope, and feeling unprepared for his change. He had been considerably alarmed, but did not seem to have a clear sense of his awful guilt in the sight of God. I read to him a Tract, prayed with him, and endeavored to persuade him of the necessity of immediate repentance.

"At the door, met a man and conversed with him; he said he thought some on the subject of religion, and knew he was a sinner. I urged him not to delay the great work of making his peace with God.

"Near a neighboring house saw four young men, who appeared very thoughtless; went to them, and told them I had a short message, which I wished them to hear and consider. After getting their attention, I told them it was, 'Prepare to meet thy God.'

"Walked to P——, and heard Rev. Mr. W. Addressed the prayer meeting in the evening, and felt some freedom. Called again on the sick man: he said he had thought much of what I said to him in the morning.

"On my way, met one of the young men whom I accosted this morning;

took him by the hand, and asked if he had thought of what I then said to him. He said he had many times during the day. Addressed him and a group of lads around him, warning them that they must awake to a sense of their danger—or perish.

"Agreed upon appointing a *Monthly Concert* for prayer, tomorrow evening, in the school-house."

"*Monday evening.* Just returned from Monthly Concert. About 40 were present. To me it was a pleasant meeting. Walked home with Mr. ———. He appeared considerably enlivened."

"*Wednesday evening.* Attended meeting at the boarding house. How much do I need pardoning and sanctifying grace."

"*Jewett City, Saturday P. M. June* 9.
(To Mrs. Page.)

"I sent yesterday to Boston for the Missionary Herald; and Esq. M——gives me the reading of the Recorder. So you see I shall not be destitute of religious intelligence. If I had a supply of Tracts, I could dispose of them here to good advantage.

"I *lose one quarter of a day this P. M.* to write and get some *rest preparatory to the Sabbath,* as I have found myself dull at meeting."

He proceeds to relate particularly the events of the preceding Sabbath, and continues the letter on Sabbath evening.

"*Thirteen* were present at the prayer-meeting this morning. I enjoyed it much. The sermon at P——, in the afternoon, was on the *duties of parents,* and uncommonly interesting.

"A Universalist preached today at the church here. So you see the enemy had the field. I do think *a faithful minister,* stationed here, might do incalculable good. It is indeed missionary ground.

"As to my own spiritual state, I can hardly tell you what it is, I find *so much impurity of motive.* I hope you have many new converts around you, and many engaged Christians. How is my own dear sister? Is she yet a Christian? Tell the dear children that Pa thinks of them, and prays for them. I hope you will make up in duties to them what has been wanting in me. Do not neglect their souls, as I have too much done,

"H. PAGE"

"*Monday, June* 11. Called on Mr. F. who is worse. He thought he had experienced a change within a few days; but I could obtain no satisfactory evidence. Endeavored to deal faithfully with him, and show him the danger of a false hope."

"*Tuesday evening.* Attended a prayer-meeting one and a half miles distant. About twenty present. I often inquire what reason I have to hope I am a Christian. I find so much selfishness in my motives to action, that I sometimes fear true love to Christ is wanting."

"*Sabbath evening, June* 17. *Twenty-one* present at the prayer-meeting at sunrise. Heard Rev. Mr. W—— morning and afternoon. Attended a prayer-meeting in the intermission. At 5 o'clock, attended the Sabbath school here; forty-two children present. This evening, prayer-meeting at the school-house. Within three days have felt uncommonly anxious for the salvation of souls; but the impenitent all around me seem yet to be thoughtless. Satan appears to be making unusual efforts. May the Lord guide me in duty. *Have I not come to this place with his glory in view?* Shall I not be the means of benefiting some souls?"

"*Friday evening,* 22. This evening, a prayer-meeting for Sabbath School teachers; about twenty attended. The meeting at the boarding-house, on Wednesday evening, was more solemn than usual. Find that some were deeply interested."

"*Wednesday evening, June* 27. Today, paid what is called 'entrance' to the work-shop, by giving Tracts to the workmen. They generally appeared pleased. Held a conversation of some length with a gentleman of considerable education. He argued on many religious subjects, and contends that man is not strictly a free agent. May God open his eyes and heart."

"*Sabbath, July* 1. About *thirty* at the morning prayer-meeting. Attended church and joined in commemorating the Lord's death at P——. At 5 P. M. attended Sabbath school, containing now upwards of *eighty* scholars, who are very regular and attentive. Yet, with all these privileges, my spiritual discernment is so dim, my affections so cold, that I must conclude I have but little real desire to 'glorify God in my body and spirit, which are his.'"

"*Wednesday evening.* Prayer-meeting solemn. More of the boarders attended than usual. One of the workmen appears to be somewhat thoughtful. Felt peculiar anxiety for the conversion of sinners."

"*Tuesday, July* 10. Last evening Capt. P—— called at my lodgings, bringing a young man seriously impressed. Found him deplorably ignorant. He was considerably affected, but did not seem to have a sense of *sin*. May God convince him, and bring him to the truth. Have just received intelligence of the death of the Rev. Dr. Worcester."

"*Saturday, July* 14. S—— H—— is hoping that he has been born again; and another, I think, gives evidence of a change. How much cause have I for humiliation, that God should use such an unworthy instrument in the conversion of sinners! And when he has, in so many instances, blessed my feeble efforts, how guilty that I am not more earnest in exertions for the good of souls!

"This afternoon learned that Mr. L—— is indulging a hope. Blessed news, that one of the workmen has been brought home to Christ!"

Encouraged by these indications, he addressed the following letter to a gentleman of much respectability, with whom he had had a friendly interview.

"Sabbath evening, 15th July.

"DEAR SIR,—Our partial acquaintance and other circumstances have led me to feel a peculiar interest in your eternal welfare. In our recent interview, I learned that you have been often affectionately reminded of the necessity of an immediate attention to the concerns of eternity, but yet that you are living without hope, and with your affections still supremely placed on earthly good.

"My feelings were not a little excited while in the house of God today, in contemplating the final separation of those who are connected by the dearest earthly ties—one to descend to the gloom of everlasting despair—the other to rise to immortal life and glory. I knew, that you had had a religious education; that a thousand prayers of pious friends had been offered in your behalf: and that a devoted wife was pouring out her intercessions to God, that you may not be separated in the future world.

"Why, Sir, this insensibility to eternal realities? Why this parleying with sin? this forgetfulness of God? this aversion to a holy life, and to the Savior of sinners? I cannot believe that your enlightened understanding will allow you to barter your soul for the trifles of earth.

"Men act in view of motives. Permit me to ask, do you not find them sufficient to induce a compliance with the simple and reasonable requisitions of the Gospel of Christ? How long, Sir, will you withhold the best affections of your heart from him who is 'the chief among ten thousands, and altogether lovely?' How long will you put far away the evil day, and slumber on the verge of ruin? How long will you, dear Sir, reject the Redeemer of mankind and his offers of eternal life? God grant that your heart may answer, 'Not a moment.' Allow me the freedom of affectionately entreating you immediately to escape from the threatened doom of the impenitent, and cast yourself as a vile rebel on the mercy of Him who alone is able to save.

"With affection and respect, sincerely yours,

"H. PAGE"

"Thursday, July 19. Felt an unusual desire this day for a revival of religion. Have conversed with L——. He appears very well. H. K. appears very solemn."

On the same day he thus wrote to Mrs. Page:

"I have received yours. Is Coventry indeed in so deplorable a condition? Where is the zeal of Christians? Is there no God? no heaven? no hell? Are there no souls on the way to death? I hoped to hear that you were enjoying a fresh anointing of the Holy Spirit. The Lord Jesus is just such a stay as you now and always need. Your companion, you will find, sooner or later, to be only a broken reed; but Christ is a safe refuge.

"We have some favorable tokens for good here. One man, Mr. L——, has obtained a hope, and is now quite active. A young woman appears today to be under convictions, and others, I think, are more solemn. As much as I desire to be with my own family, *I should not dare to leave this place at this time.* I hope that God has sent me here to be a means of advancing his cause. I felt yesterday a peculiar anxiety for sinners, and think I was enabled to maintain, in a degree, a praying spirit.

"In all your trials, you will find it sweet casting yourself into the arms of Christ. He is ready to grant consolation to his children. Only put your confidence in Him, and be active and faithful in his service.

Yours with sincere affection,

"H. PAGE"

"*Sabbath, July* 22. At the prayer-meeting this morning, learned that H. K. had found peace in believing. In the evening had a long conversation with the family of Mr. ——. Found one of his daughters strongly attached to dancing, and, in the pursuit of vanity, waiting for God to do his work in her heart. Endeavored to take away her excuses, and convince her that the guilt is all her own. May the Holy Spirit set home truth to her heart.

"*July* 28. This day completes thirty years of my life. How ought I to begin this new year for God?

"*August* 2. Compelled by pain in my breast to leave work in the shop; painted a landscape view of the factory. Attended a meeting to devise means for *obtaining a faithful minister* to be settled and devote his labors constantly in the village.

"*August* 4. Health more feeble, and obliged to resort to medicine. In addition to my bodily infirmities, I find great languor in my spiritual affections. O for a more ardent desire to be instrumental in promoting the glory of God! May I not, blessed Jesus, leave myself with thee? Wilt thou not guide me, and lead me back to thy fold, and make me faithful the short time I have to continue on earth? Thou knowest my weakness, my instability, my dim vision of eternal things, and my ingratitude. Pardon my wanderings, revive my languid affections, and fit me for all thy pleasure."

Here closes the little journal he kept of his brief stay in Jewett City; and we regret to say, he has left behind him *nothing further in the shape of a journal.* Had he made and preserved even such hasty notices of his efforts from day to day, and the blessing that followed them, it is only known to God how extensively the record of them might have been blessed in inciting others to duty.

On the last page of the journal we have a memorandum of *"Books out,"* including Baxter's Call, and a few works of kindred character, the loaning of which, as he judged them adapted to the state of particular individuals, was one of his accustomed means of usefulness.

From another memorandum, it appears, that, while he was performing the labors of love above recounted, he worked *fifty-seven days, at seventy-five cents a day.* Here was a mechanic, performing his daily task on hire; establishing and sustaining a religious meeting at the boarding-house, on Wednesday evenings; a meeting of the people of God for prayer, on Sabbath mornings, at sunrise; and, though he went about three miles to attend public worship, throwing his efforts into a Sabbath school at 5 P. M., and instructing a class; devoting Sabbath evenings to meetings and family visitation; conversing with the sick, the careless, the anxious, and those indulging a hope; distributing Tracts; endeavoring to awaken an interest in the benevolent operations of the day; keeping a brief diary; abounding in prayer; and adopting, with others, incipient measures (which proved successful) for the formation of a church and the settlement of an evangelical pastor. Many a professed Christian, as he goes out on a journey, or to tarry among strangers, "leaves his religion behind him." Not so our brother: "I hope," was his language, "that *God has sent me here to advance his cause.*"

The friend with whom he lodged says, religion was always first in his mind. If he entered a family, after the usual salutations, this subject was immediately introduced. In promoting the Sabbath schools, he would go out into the highways; and wherever he found those of suitable age, however far from God they might seem, would gain their attention, and, if possible, bring them in. Six or eight wild boys, from twelve to seventeen years old, were thus induced to attend; were led to see their ruin by sin, and brought hopefully to Christ. Some of them became teachers in the school. One of them, a little before the death of Mr. Page, expressed an earnest desire to see him; and said that, but for his efforts, he must have been, to all human view, an eternal outcast. The meetings in the boarding-house were continued about a year after he left us, and the saving influences of the Holy Spirit descended upon them. The gentleman whom he addressed by letter, July 15, publicly professed Christ, and frequently spoke of Mr. Page's faithful efforts for his salvation. A daughter of one of the families he visited, lamented on her death-bed that she had not heeded his admonitions. 'Oh,'

said she, 'that I could see that Mr. Page! O that I had regarded his warnings!' At the close of the evening he often spent much time in his chamber
before retiring to rest, sometimes till a late hour, doubtless wrestling with
God in prayer for the individuals with whom, during the day, he had been
conversing.

We now return with our brother to his peaceful home, where his health
for several weeks continued feeble, and forbade his returning to labor at
Jewett City, as he had intended. But it appears that, though in "much debil-
ity of body," and for a time "unable to converse much," he did not relin-
quish the one prime object of his life. On the 18th of August he thus wrote
to C. H. H. a young lady who had been for some time anxious for her soul.

"According to your own confession, your case is deplorable indeed.
Convinced of the necessity of religion, and of the vanity of all earthly pur-
suits, you still choose the way to death. But stop; is C——a in the way to
death? can it be possible that she has lived three months sensible of her
danger, and knowing her duty, without casting herself, a guilty rebel, at the
foot of the cross? O remember, the Savior will not always call. Continuing
to reject him, the day of your calamity is at hand! The eternal sorrows that
shall come upon you, make haste. Think again of his melting invitations:
'Look unto me, and be ye saved.' 'Ho, every one that thirsteth, come ye to
the waters.' Slighting such calls, and abusing such privileges as you enjoy,
must you not deserve and receive an aggravated doom? If these were the
last words I could ever speak to you, I would say, *Haste—throw yourself
immediately on the mercy of God in Christ.* Unless you do this, you can
never enter heaven; and unless you do it *soon*, it is more than probable the
lamentation will be yours: 'the harvest is past, the summer ended—and I
am not saved!'"

On the 23rd of August he wrote an affectionate letter to friends in Jewett
City, expressing his regret that he was unable to return; encouraging them
to persevere in duty; and enclosing a solemn appeal to his Sabbath school
class.

September 5, he transmitted, for publication in the Guardian, a sketch
of the interview held with a young lady, July 22; his object being "to convince her that there was *no obstacle on the part of God* to her coming to
him, and that the guilt of her continued impenitence rested *wholly and
alone* on herself.

"'I acknowledge,' she said, 'that I do love the pleasures of this world;
and that *dancing*, which is my favorite amusement, is one of the last things
I could give up.'

"'Are you prepared then,' I asked, 'to risk your eternal all, for a short season of this world's enjoyment? When so much has been done for your salvation, will you still hazard the tremendous consequences of being 'a lover of pleasure more than a lover of God?'"

"'However that may be,' said she, 'I shall continue in my present course till the Spirit of God leads me to think and feel differently. Should I die now, I know I must be lost; but I can see no way to prevent it. I do not desire to be miserable—I wish to go to heaven as well as others; but what can I do? The *prayer* of the wicked is "abomination to the Lord;" and if I am to be saved, when God sees fit to change my heart, he will do it.'

"'True,' said I, 'the sacrifice of the wicked is abomination to the Lord,' he neither accepts nor requires it. He requires the prayer of 'a broken and contrite spirit;' and you can render no valid excuse for not going to him this day, and even this moment, with a spirit contrite and broken for sin. Every moral exercise of your heart, and every act of your life, that are not consistent with supreme love to God, are also an abomination in his sight. And besides all this, your impenitence and your neglect of religion is *your own choice;* for this you are guilty; and for this, if persisted in, you will be justly condemned. If you cannot plead this excuse at the bar of God, never, I beseech you, make it again on earth.

"After endeavoring in vain to obtain a promise that she would do so much for her salvation, as for a short season each day to call to mind and *confess her sins individually to God,* I left her, hoping that the interview would be the means at least of exciting some serious reflections.

"I think we see in this example, that impenitent sinners have *no desire to become the followers of Christ.* They wish to escape misery, and to be happy; but are unwilling humbly to accept of Christ; and refuse to engage, for his sake, in self-denying duty. They also, impliedly, if not confessedly, cast the *blame of their impenitence on God.*

"*Let every Christian,* while so many are thus excusing and deluding themselves, be faithful in unveiling to them the real state of their hearts, and showing them their guilt and danger. Let him warn them no longer to reply against God; show them that their excuses arise from hatred to him and his perfect law, and from their own disposition to justify themselves. And let him add to this, frequent and fervent prayer, that their eyes may be opened, and that they may cast themselves on the mercy of God in Christ.

"To *persons of the character of the young lady above described,* I would say, in the language of the apostle, that, at the bar of judgment, 'every mouth will be stopped, and all the world become guilty before God.' At that dread tribunal you can plead no palliation for your impenitent life. You must stand confounded, while you acknowledge the justice of the sentence that fixes your doom in eternal wo. Be deceived no longer. Your immortal soul is at stake. Awake now to your danger, while you are in a land of hope. Acknowledge yourself a vile and guilty rebel; and remember that *you must repent and believe in Christ*, or you can never be admitted to the abodes of the blessed."

There stands appended to a copy of this article the following note, dated 1829, in the hand-writing of Mr. Page:

"The young lady above described received impressions from this article which resulted in her hopeful conversion to God. She has since died, trusting in the merits of Christ."

"Coventry, September 20, 1821.
(To Miss J. B.)

"I hear you *have not yet professed Christ before men*. If you hope that you are a child of God, I think you would receive much spiritual benefit, and be instrumental of more good to others, by publicly joining yourself to his people.

"The field is open to all who are willing to labor in it; and the present is a day when none can excuse themselves for being inactive. Every humble, well-directed effort for Zion's cause, God seems ready to own and bless. This is also an age and country in which *females* may do much to advance the Redeemer's kingdom.

"And now, Miss J——, can you not do more than you have done? Is there no Christian female, whom you can encourage? no impenitent sinner whom you can warn of his danger? no young friend whom you might hope to bring to the knowledge of the truth? Do be faithful to the youth around you. Pray for them, and labor with them, that they receive not the doom of the rejecters of Christ.

"Your friend,

"H. PAGE"

"Coventry, Monday evening, 8 *Oct.* 1821.
(To Miss P—— A——.)

"MY DEAR FRIEND,—This afternoon we have committed to the dust the body of one of your intimate acquaintances, D. R. Why was it not myself? Why was it not my friend P——? We are still in the land of the living, and God grant that the remainder of our days may be spent in the service of Christ.

"What are your feelings, my friend, as you revert to those seasons *when the Holy Spirit spoke to your conscience*, and brought you, in some degree, to feel your wretched condition? Are all serious impressions banished from your mind? Are the Divine influences withdrawn for ever? Is my friend, who was once trembling in view of her state as a sinner, now thoughtlessly pursuing her course to the world of wo? I can hardly bear the thought. An immortal being—blessed with a religious education—a child of many prayers, labors and tears—continuing to reject the offers of life, and refuse the gracious calls of a bleeding Savior!

"May I not indulge the hope, that, ere this, you are a child of God; an active laborer in his vineyard; and prepared for the rest that 'remains for the people of God?' If not, let me affectionately urge you *now to awake;* to delay the work of repentance no longer; and to suffer the enemy of souls to gain no farther advantage, lest it prove your eternal ruin.

"Do not remain careless because others are so. Be an active friend of Christ yourself, and labor to bring them to be so too.

"I have been *but little acquainted with the state of the youth* among us, the summer past, having been for some time absent; and for the last two months *my health has been so much impaired that I have had opportunity to converse with but few.* But there is reason to fear that many are gliding down to the gates of death.

"This may be the last time that I shall ever address you on this subject; but when we meet at the bar of God, may it appear that these lines, and our opportunities of conversation, have not been in vain. Will you not write and tell me the state of your mind? I did intend to have seen you again before you left Coventry, but was disappointed.

"Your affectionate friend,

"H. Page"

On the 15th of March, 1822, he writes to H—— D——, a young relative, *on business;* and that part of the letter being finished, proceeds to express his regret that their personal interview, when his friend was at Coventry, was so short; and his hope that correspondence may be an acceptable and useful substitute. "A thousand topics of interest," he says, "present themselves; but all others sink into insignificance compared with eternal realities.

"And now, dear cousin, permit me to speak to you particularly on *your own spiritual state.* From your conversation I was led to conclude that you did not consider yourself as having experienced that change 'from death unto life,' which the Scriptures represent as indispensable to salvation. 'Without holiness no man shall see the Lord!' Destitute of supreme love to God, our state is indeed deplorable. While we are purposing at some future time to give him our hearts, an unexpected and unwelcome messenger cuts short our hopes for ever.

"I can assure you, my friend, that no period of life will ever be so favorable for your accepting the offers of mercy as the present. God has said, 'I love them that love me, and they that seek me early shall find me.' I would affectionately urge you, by all that is solemn in heaven, on earth, and in the world of despair; in a dying bed, and in the day of judgment; to delay the work of preparation for death no longer. Hasten, and flee to Christ as a ruined sinner. Days and months fly swiftly; all opportunity to make your peace with God will soon be over; and the soul once lost, is lost for ever.

"Do write me, and fully express your feelings.

"Your affectionate friend and cousin,

"H. PAGE"

The following is an illustration of a final and almost desperate effort to reach the heart of one whose case seemed nearly hopeless.

(To Miss N—— R——.)

"The remark has often been made, that 'it will do no good to converse with N—— R—— on her state as a sinner;' and you have probably yourself been brought to the same conclusion.

"I take my pen to say a few words more to you, trembling lest it should only be the means of hardening you in sin. All motives from this world would lead me at once to desist. But when I look to a dying hour, and a little beyond, into an unchanging eternity, I feel irresistibly impelled once more to expostulate with a perishing fellow-sinner. I beg you to receive it in kindness, and as probably the last lines or words, addressed to you personally, which you will ever read or hear from me while you continue professedly the enemy of God.

"And now, what shall I say? Will you accompany me to that silent room? Here lies a young lady wasted by disease, and just on the confines of eternity. Approach her—the paleness of death is on her cheek. Take her by the hand—why start at its icy coldness? It is but kindred dust. Listen to her tale. 'Alas! my friend, I am dying! I am dying! My day of grace is over. My sands are almost run. In a few moments I shall be enveloped in devouring fire. I have lived in sin, rejected Christ, and now he hides his face from me, and there is no remedy. O how have Christians plead with me to make God my portion; but I would not listen. I accused God of injustice, quarreled with that sovereign love that would have wooed my heart; resisted the Holy Spirit, that was teaching me my lost condition and pressing me to accept of Christ. He called, but I refused; and now he is withdrawn from me for ever. O my friend, take warning from me. While you have the offers of mercy, flee to Christ. Make haste. Delay not a moment, lest you mingle your cries with me in the bottomless pit!'

"Can you look at this melancholy picture and not apply it to yourself? Death is even now at the door. There is no time to parley with Satan, or your own heart. Heaven must be gained soon, or not at all. Christ now stands at the door and knocks. O, N——! say not again, depart!

"That you may bid him a cordial welcome, is the earnest wish and prayer of your affectionate friend,

"H. PAGE"

Early in the autumn of 1822, commenced another precious revival of religion, which continued for several months, as the result of which, he says, in a letter to his cousin H—— D——, near the close of winter, "about *one hundred* have obtained a hope. Some of the most amiable have found their hearts violently opposed to God; have even represented themselves as 'devils incarnate;' and found peace only in confessing all their awful guilt, and casting themselves alone on the merits and mercy of Christ." In a subsequent letter to Mrs. A—— A——, a distant friend, he gives the names of twenty-five, with whom she was acquainted, who had united with the church.

This is all the notice he has left of what he did, or felt; of his prayers, or labors, or success, or thanksgivings, during this blessed harvest of souls, a season in which he rejoiced, as fraught with the choicest of all blessings conferred by a gracious God this side of heaven. A friend, who knew him well, states that, in this revival, he manifested a deeper interest, and put forth more glowing and unceasing efforts than ever before. Religious meetings were held almost daily, and sometimes at different hours of the same day; and usually he attended them *all. Personal conversation with individuals*—the careless, the inquiring, and the young convert—was, in connection with prayer, the prominent means of his usefulness; and for this, as opportunity offered, and duty seemed to call, he did not hesitate, at any and all times, to leave his business. Though he had little of this world's goods, it was generally true, that he "owed no man any thing;" the necessary wants of his family were supplied; he felt that, while the influences of the Holy Spirit were descending, the opportunity must be improved to pluck the golden fruit; and that, whether he obtained a little more, or a little less of this world's goods was nothing, compared with the salvation of a soul. If any would censure his course, let the decision be deferred till the judgment day. And O that he may not then be found *almost alone*—with a *little band*, who supremely devoted themselves, while in this world, FIRST to glorify God in the salvation of souls around them, and AFTER THAT to make provision for the present life.

In reference to Mr. Page's efforts, at this season, the individual to whom his last moving appeal above quoted was addressed, relates the following incidents: "I had long been awakened, but determined to let no one know it; and made every effort to *escape Mr. Page*. At length, near the close of November, I attended a little meeting where I believe all were indulging a hope, except my brother and myself. After conversing with my brother, he came to me, and wished me to tell him the state of my mind. I at first said that I was in despair; but from the manner of his reply, perceived that he did not give full credit to my assertion. This roused my resentment, and I at once determined not to speak again while he remained in the room. He pressed me to decide that I would, without delay, give my heart to Christ; but I was so angry that I would not even answer him. This conversation brought the malignity of my heart more clearly to my own view than I had ever seen it before. I could never have imagined myself to have indulged such malice as I then felt towards him; and my misery was, that I could assign no other reason for it but his faithfulness. Soon, as I trust, God was pleased to subdue my enmity; and my hatred to Mr. Page was *at once changed to love, for I saw in him the image of my blessed Redeemer."*

A little phrase incidentally dropped by his pastor, as from his window he saw him approaching in company with another, has a significant import: *"There comes Mr. Page with another lamb."* Seeing *him* come with an individual beside him in that season of mercy, such a result, it seems, was the first thing anticipated.

CHAPTER 5

His narrative of Thomas Hamitah Patoo, a native of the Marquesas Islands, hopefully brought to Christ in Coventry.

Though Mr. Page left no written memorial of his efforts, or the state of his mind during the work of grace just alluded to, the deficiency is at least partially supplied in the interesting memoir of Thomas Hamitah Patoo, which he originally prepared. He had often agitated the question, whether, even at his age, and with a rising family around him, it was not his duty to go and labor in some humble station among the heathen; and when Patoo was located near him, he felt that *Providence had brought a heathen to his own door,* and that he must omit no efforts for his salvation.

Patoo had reached the age of about fourteen, when, attracted by ships which occasionally touched at his native Islands, he resolved to visit America; and to secure his purpose, jumped on board a ship with her sails spread, just in time to see his afflicted father reluctantly wave his handkerchief as a signal of farewell. He arrived at Boston; and after a varied life of two or three years, and many sufferings occasioned by his own folly, was taken under the charge of Mr. D—— H——, a benevolent gentleman, who, in May, 1822, placed him in a pious family in Coventry, commending him to "the prayers and Christian kindness of the pastor and the whole church."

"At *a prayer-meeting at sunrise*, in the autumn of 1822," says the narrative, "it was observed that Thomas was much affected, and wept bitterly. He was made a subject of special prayer; and his conversation at the close of the meeting, evidently showed that he was under the strivings of the Holy Spirit." These impressions were deepened by the clear exhibition of truth at successive meetings, and its faithful personal application to himself in private conversation. His distress was such one day, that he left home in the rain, first to find his Christian friend, and then to visit his pastor, to obtain some relief. Truth presented, took hold of his mind; but he rebelled against

God; murmured at the conversion of a young acquaintance; and returned to spend a sleepless night, in view of his hopeless condition. On the day following, his anxiety continued unabated; his distress was such that he could not attend to the business assigned him; most of the day was spent in agonizing prayer; till at length the Savior appeared for him, his burdened conscience was relieved, and he found peace in believing. His own narrative of the way in which he was led, expressed in his broken idiom, is a delightful exemplification of the power and excellency of true religion.

"*Question.* Thomas, what was the state of your mind after the commencement of the revival in Coventry?

"*Answer.* Christians talk to me a great deal about my bad heart. Me think my heart good enough.

"*Question.* Did you then endeavor to pray?

"*Answer.* Mrs. T. teach me to say Lord's prayer. I think me got no mother, no father, no sister, no brother here; and Mrs. T. good to me, so I do as she tell me. Then I kneel down before I go to bed, and say prayer.

"*Question.* Did you occasionally omit this duty?

"*Answer.* Sometimes. Then Deacon T. say you must say your prayers, Thomas, every night. Then me go pray mad.

"*Question.* Had you any different feelings at the morning prayer-meeting, at which you wept?

"*Answer.* Then me feel heavy—feel afraid to die—feel sorry for my sin. Me try to pray, 'Our Father.' Me go home, think what minister say, then I pray. Next day forget it all—then feel light.

"*Question.* When you went to the inquiry meetings, how did you feel?

"*Answer.* I feel good some—then I feel heavy again. When minister say all about poor sinner—then I feel sorry.

"*Question.* What were your feelings at the meeting for inquiry on Sabbath evening?

"*Answer.* Heart feel hard. Somebody tell me J. B. got a new heart. I feel angry.

"*Question.* How did you spend the Tuesday following?

"*Answer.* Me want to see minister. I set out—go part way, feel so bad can go no further—then kneel down by a great rock and pray. Me say, O Lord, have mercy on poor Thomas, poor heathen—give him new heart—take away old heart—O give him new heart now. Then I go on. Go in minister's barn—'fraid to go in house—then I pray again. Then look round and say, God make this hay—this grain—all these things—why can't God make me new heart. Me wipe tears off my cheeks, but they come again. Then go in house. Mrs. C. say, What the matter, Thomas, you hurt you? I so 'shamed, me say, O it rains out doors. Want to have her think it rain on my face.

"*Question.* What did you say to the minister?

"*Answer.* Me say, me got that bad heart yet.

"*Question.* Did you feel glad when told that J. B. had a new heart?

"*Answer.* No, sir, me feel bad—me feel very heavy—me want to come first, before any body get in. When me go away, hope me come to be like J. B.

"*Question.* How did you feel that night and the day following?

"*Answer.* That night me feel heavy—heavy all over. Eyes all tears—could no sleep. Next day feel so all time. Afternoon go work in barn with W.—could no work. Feel me want to pray. Tell W. we kneel down. Then me say, O Lord have mercy on poor Thomas, poor W.—give us new hearts. Then me think about Jesus Christ, and about Christian folks. Me never feel so before. Heavy all gone. Then me love to pray, and say Our Father, and thank great God he give J. B. a new heart. Then me think me feel to love Christ—me go up on hay to find him—pray to him. Then me think Christ every where. Then come down.

"*Question.* What were your feelings during the meeting in the evening?

"*Answer.* Me want to shake hand with the minister, then feel to love all Christians.

"*Question.* How do you think you know a Christian from an impenitent sinner?

"*Answer.* Christian shake hand hard—his hand feel warm—sinner no shake hand.

"*Question.* What do you mean by a new heart?

"*Answer.* A heart that feel to love good thought.

"*Question.* How do you know your heart to be soft now?

"*Answer.* Why, me no feel mad to any body; if man strike me, no want to strike him back again.

"After his conversion, his advancement in divine knowledge was rapid. The Holy Spirit seemed to teach him to understand the truths of God, and as far as understood, they evidently produced the fruits of holiness."

He had a great desire to unite with the church at the approaching communion, and when the pastor informed him that, at the suggestion of his distant friend, it was thought best that his admission be deferred, he replied with great feeling: "If, Sir, you think best, then me wait; but maybe me die soon—then me never own Christ before men!"

He adorned the Christian character—loved the Bible—prayed much, especially for his own relatives and countrymen, for the heathen, and the impenitent in Christian lands—and, like the brother who made him the object of his Christian love and more than paternal regard, and wrote his history, he *put forth his most ardent efforts to bring sinners to Christ*. The statements in the two following communications are full of import, and have an impressive bearing on the immediate object of this work. The first is from a young lady, who had long been convicted of sin, and was still cherishing a rebellious heart.

"'After our friend Thomas indulged a hope, I endeavored,' she says, 'to avoid him as much as possible; but one day, after conversing with my sister, and expressing much joy because she got a new heart, he turned to me and said, "N——, why you no give up that bad heart—why you no come with C. and be a Christian? Me want you be a Christian too!" In order to evade what he said, and prevent his saying more, I replied, "Thomas, why did you never speak to me about those things before? Perhaps, had you been as faithful in talking to me, as you have been to my sister, I too should have had a new heart." With an expression of deep regret, he replied, "N——, me very sorry me no talk to you before. Me *pray* for you before, and *now* me talk to you." After this he embraced every opportunity of affectionately urging upon me immediate submission to Christ.

"'In the height of the revival, when a number of Christian friends were spending the day at our house, feeling no disposition to be with them, I retired to another room, and there staid meditating on my hopeless condition. It was not long before some one rapped at the door, and who was it but Thomas! He immediately began, in the most feeling manner, to entreat me to submit to Christ without delay. "Christ ready to receive you—all the good Christians want you to come—angel in heaven ready to rejoice over you— why you no come?" After conversing in this manner for some minutes, he was silent. At length, looking at me most expressively, he said, "Me sorry me no talk to you before. Me pray for you; me want to pray *with* you." We knelt, and Thomas poured forth the feelings of his heart in language like this: "O mercy, Father, have mercy on us sinners. Have mercy on this friend. Pray this friend may now give up that bad heart to Christ, and not go to hell," etc. It was the burden of his prayer, that I might then submit to Christ. I will leave others to judge what were my feelings, to have this heathen, who had but just learned there was a God, on his knees pleading for mercy on me, a stubborn sinner, hardened under the meridian light of the Gospel.'"

The other communication to which we have referred, is from one *now a minister of the Gospel,* and was made to Mr. Page a few months previous to his death:

"'The first time I saw Thomas after he thought he had been born again, was on Sabbath, Dec. 8, 1822. I was then groaning under convictions of sin—I felt myself lost. It seemed that there was but a step between me and hell. I longed to converse with some one, but I was too proud to tell any one how I felt.

"'Thus situated, Thomas approached me, and began to question me about my spiritual condition. I told him I felt that there was no hope for me: I had sinned against so much light, and so many strivings of the Spirit.

"'He proceeded to urge me to immediate submission. "Why you no give up that bad heart? It will do you no good to keep it. It will destroy you for ever. Give it up *now* to Christ. Christ ready to give you a new, a good heart. Me hope me have given my bad heart to him. Me hope me have a new one. Oh, sir, do give up your bad heart."

"'I told him I wished I could, but it was so hard I could not: something was in the way, I did not know what.

"'This excuse did not satisfy him. It only led him to press home with more earnestness the duty of immediately giving up my *bad heart* to Christ.

"'I felt so distressed, I begged him to pray for me. This was the first time in my life that I ever had made such a request, and the very asking him to pray for me deepened my impressions. It came to my mind immediately, "What! must you, a gospel-hardened rebel, call in to your help the prayers of a poor Marquesan, who has but just been converted from the worship of idols! He has just now heard of Christ, and received him as his Savior; you have heard of him for years, and have been slighting his salvation, despising his offers of mercy, trampling on his blood, and grieving his Spirit!" These reflections were like daggers to my soul.

"'Thomas promised to pray for me, but left me saying, *"Oh, Sir, give up that bad heart* NOW." This sentence was the most powerful sermon I ever heard; it contained the eloquence of the Spirit; and coming in the way it did, with an expression of the most tender pity and concern, left an impression on my mind which, I trust, will never be effaced. I have always considered his earnest exhortation to me at that time, as *the principal means in the hand of God of my conversion.*'"

In March, 1823, Mr. Page accompanied Patoo to the Foreign Mission School, then in operation in Cornwall, where he hoped to become qualified to return as a messenger of Christ to his native islands. On the 30th of March he thus wrote to Mr. Page:

"MY DEAR CHRISTIAN FRIEND—I have received your very kind letter, and am now happy to answer it. One of my brothers writes for me, because I can't write well enough yet. I tell him what to write, so the word be some like Thomas. I very glad the great God in heaven make the Coventry people pray for poor heathen where there is no Savior. I think they pray for me too, that I be prepared to tell the heathen all about the great God, and our Savior Jesus Christ. I rejoice a great deal to hear about sinner come to Christ, and get a new heart. I hope the good work continue always among you, so I rejoice always. The people here have no revival—no pray enough. I sorry; I hope we pray enough by and by. We have good many meetings, but no feel.

"I hope I go home by and by, and have sinner come to God in my country. Yes, my dear Mr. Page, *I go, if I live to be ready*. We have some scholars no love the Savior. I tell them they must be born again or go to hell. I talk to some sinner all about they no come to Christ. I tell them I come away from heathen land, and find a good Savior; they been here so long, and no come to Christ. You must pray a great deal for poor sinners in Cornwall school. May be we have a revival here.

"I must close now. I think I pray every day for you and all my friends. The great God bless you and make you do good while you live, and when you and I die, may we meet and *shake hand in heaven*, and stay always with our Savior and all who love him.

"Your true friend,

"Patoo"

This promising youth, in the mysterious providence of God, was called, on the 9th of June following, to join the lamented Henry Oobookiah in a better world. As he stood with Mr. Page over Oobookiah's grave, in Cornwall, three months before, he said, with great solemnity, *"May be I lie here too."* He remained steadfast, and in sickness and death gave delightful evidence of Divine support. Further particulars may be learned from the memoir, which is published by the American Tract Society.

In the journey to Cornwall with Patoo, Mr. Page passed a Sabbath in Torringford with the venerable father of Samuel J. Mills, whose name is so dear to all the friends of Missions. He attended the religious meetings of the congregation; and feeling a deep interest that the work of God should be revived among them, on returning to Coventry, engaged Christians to pray for them, and wrote to the family of Mr. Mills an affectionate letter.

In their reply, they say: "We hope we shall ever have reason for gratitude, that Providence directed your steps here, and gave you an opportunity to address this people. There seemed to be a general impression that day, that God was about to visit us again. Christians began to feel that they must sleep no longer, and that something must be done. The next Sabbath evening, though the weather was very unfavorable, five of the brethren called unexpectedly to spend a little season in prayer, and we have not, for many months, witnessed so much solemnity. Last evening we had twice the number, and evidently increasing fervor, and one instance of awakening was reported.

"We mention these circumstances that you may know our state, as you manifested a deep interest in our spiritual welfare; and to engage a renewed interest in your prayers."

CHAPTER 6

CLOSE OF HIS LABORS IN COVENTRY.

In the summer of 1823 he had another violent attack of fever, with a renewed inflammation of the liver, by which he was brought, as he and those around him supposed, to the last moments of life. "He was calm," says one who watched at his bed side, "but did not receive such measures of grace as were imparted to him when God's time had come for him to die." Thus did his Heavenly Father see fit again to discipline him for further usefulness.

On regaining essentially his health, he was induced to direct his attention chiefly to the business of engraving, which led to his being employed for a time by the American Tract Society, then existing at Boston. We find him, on the 17th July, 1824, in the Museum of the "Society of Inquiry respecting Missions, in the Theological Seminary at Andover," writing a description of some of the interesting objects before him, for the benefit of the Sabbath School he had left in Coventry.

"Missionary Room, Theol. Sem. Andover.
(To the Members of the First Sabbath School Class.)

"MY DEAR FRIENDS,—With no less than six gods of the heathen staring me in the face, I am now seated to redeem my pledge of a letter. One of these gods is from the Sandwich Islands, and was worshipped by Tamahamaha, the queen; and though larger, is similar to the one in New-Haven, a picture of which you have seen.

"The remainder are Hindoo gods. One from Bengal is in the form of a man, about twelve inches high, painted white, with tinsel around the shoulders, waist, wrists and ankles, having the appearance of gold and silver, with red and green colors intermingled. Its hair resembles the fibres of the black ostrich feather, and on its head is a small cap. It would, in short, make a beautiful doll; yet, this is none other than the famous god Vishnu, which human beings like ourselves worship.

"The next is Krishnu, the god of music, a favorite god of the Indian women. It is about ten inches in height, perfectly black, and with its arms in the position of playing on an instrument.

"The other three are brass, five or six inches high, representing the god Vishnu in different incarnations. The head and body are like a man, with four arms, while the lower part of one terminates in a fish, and of another in a tortoise. In such odious forms the Hindoos believe their gods descended to the earth. How is it possible that the mind of man can be so debased as to pay homage to such horrid objects?

"I now turn with pleasure to the *Ollas,* or palm leaves, on which are written the Gospels of Matthew and Mark in Cingalese, presented by our Missionaries in Ceylon. The leaves are about fourteen inches long and two wide, straight and smooth, written very handsomely on both sides, in perfectly straight lines. Perhaps these two Gospels fill one hundred and fifty of the leaves, which are connected by strings passing through them, so that they can be opened and read, or folded very compactly together in a small bundle. Another is 'Devout Meditations in Tamul,' written on the olla by a native convert of Swartz, and is used as a school-book on the Malabar coast. It was presented by Christian David, from whom we have had many interesting communications.

"I next look at the *ear-rings*, which were given by Catharine Brown to aid the Palestine Mission, and were redeemed by some ladies and placed here; valued at sixteen dollars. Happy would it be, should many of *our* females cast their useless ornaments into the treasury of the Lord. By this means alone, *many*, now enveloped in pagan darkness, might be brought to rejoice in the light and salvation of our God. Catharine *worked while it was day*, and is now gone to her rest.

"I here see also a *twig* from a tree over the grave of Harriet Newell. Though her precious dust there moulders in a pagan land, she will never regret—no, *never*—the greatest of her sacrifices for a perishing world.

"While sitting here, I cannot but reflect on the deplorable condition of those who have not the Gospel. Contrast our situation with theirs, and it seems a paradise. Let us do *all in our power*, that the news of a Savior may be soon extended to every corner of the globe.

"I left you, my friends, with regret. I hope you are all making advances in holiness, as well as in Divine knowledge. Live not, my friends, as do others. Be *eminently* devoted to God. Let the lukewarm Christian be severely reproved when he beholds your life, and the sinner plainly discern the difference between 'him that serveth God and him that serveth Him not.' Then will your life be happy, and at death you shall enter into the joy of your Lord.

"A work of grace seems to be silently progressing in this place, and a powerful revival has recently commenced in Salem. Pray for me.

"Your affectionate friend,

"H. PAGE"

To a young lady of a family in which he some weeks resided, he wrote the following awakening note:

Sabbath evening, Sept. 19, 1824.

"MY FRIEND M—— lives, I fear, alas! without hope, and without God in the world. No title to a heavenly inheritance; no Savior to cheer her in sorrow; none on whom to lean when nature is dissolving; none to welcome her to the abodes of the blessed.

"Is such the deplorable state of the friend I am addressing? Ah, M——, your prospects are gloomy indeed! A few more days of delay, and your probation is closed; hope dies; and a long eternity will echo and re-echo, WRATH TO COME—WRATH TO COME.

"The less feeling you may have on this subject, the more alarming your condition. Up, then, M——, and flee for life. There is not a moment to be lost. While you wait, your sins are increasing; the Savior is rejected, the Holy Spirit resisted; and there is reason to fear he will leave you for ever. Now what is your decision? What course, M——, will you take? Now salvation is offered. The door of mercy is open, after so many years spent in sin. Come, I entreat you, as a penitent prodigal, and cast yourself on the mercy of an injured and bleeding Savior.

Your friend and well-wisher,

"H. PAGE"

The following is the last letter which has come to hand, written previous to his leaving Coventry:

"Coventry, Friday P. M. Nov. 26, 1824.
(To C—— B——.)

"As I take my pen, I call to mind that once you indulged the hope that you were a friend of God, and even contemplated uniting with the visible church. What, C——, is now the state of your soul?

"Am I then addressing an impenitent sinner? If so, what shall I say? The exhortations you received while under the strivings of the Spirit, can hardly have ceased ringing in your ears. The threatenings of Jehovah, and a long catalogue of sins, still lie against you. An opening eternity and a judgment day are just before you—and here you live on the forbearance of God, with no Savior to befriend you, and no Holy Spirit to console you; and all your life, through fear of death, subject to bondage. Your case, my friend, is deplorable indeed; and in view of it, what will you do? Will you still give no listening ear to the tender expostulations of a dying Savior? Will you continue to grieve that Holy Comforter by whose influence alone you can be saved? Will you not stop, C——, and make the interests of your soul the first object of your life? Wait not for another revival of religion. Before it shall arrive the monument of death may tell the passing stranger: 'Here lies C—— B——.' Now is your best—perhaps your only time. Let me affectionately urge you, by all the motives which can be drawn from heaven, earth and hell, to escape for your life. After waiting so long, Christ is still willing to receive you as a humble penitent trusting in his mercy, and in no other character can you ever be saved. Methinks, while you read, you will come to the resolution, that, let others do what they will, you 'will serve the Lord.' Do you resolve thus? God and yourself only know.

"Affectionately yours,

"H. Page"

Mr. Page's connection with the Tract Society at Boston, led to his appointment as Depositary of the American Tract Society, formed at New York in the spring of 1825. A few items of his history, previous to his leaving his native place, remain yet to be gathered.

"During the eight years that he passed under my ministry," says his respected pastor, "he exhibited much decision of religious character, and much zeal and activity in the cause of Christ. Uncontrollable providences only could keep him from the house of God, where he performed a prominent part in his praises, and in the instruction of the Sabbath School. Very few sermons were preached on the Sabbath, or on week days, which he did not hear, and the plans of which he did not preserve in writing. In seasons of the special outpouring of the Holy Spirit, he was one of the first to 'hear a sound of going in the tops of the mulberry trees,' and to bestir himself. He was in the conference and prayer-meetings, and his voice was heard in earnest supplication for the conversion of sinners.

"He would converse faithfully with the careless, and search out and report to the pastor those who were seriously impressed. In the examination of candidates for admission to the church, *not unfrequent references were made to his conversation* as a means of awakening their attention; and there is evidence that he contributed an important instrumentality in the conversion of many sinners. In seasons of spiritual declension he did not feel that direct efforts for the conversion of men might be omitted; and though few attended the prayer-meetings, he was sure to be one. If a little company united in concert prayer, or private prayer, he was among them. For a long period, three or four brethren, of whom he was one, devoted one evening in each week to prayer in the meeting-house, where, in secret, and without light for the natural eye, they supplicated the descent of the Spirit. Neither the members of the church nor the pastor knew of the meeting, till, at the approach of winter, it was transferred to his study; they received a large accession to their number; were cheered with the special presence of the Comforter, and it proved *the commencement of an interesting revival of religion.*

"In seasons of stupidity, brother Page found individuals in whose spiritual welfare he manifested much interest by conversing and praying with them; and his labors in this respect were not in vain in the Lord. From the time of his conversion, so long as a resident here, he was *ardent, active, and untiring;* this characterizes the man; and his efforts were *principally directed to one object—the conversion of sinners.*"

A valuable friend, (Mr. D—— W——,) who was very intimate with Mr. Page, says, that, at the close of religious meetings, his mind would often become *intensely fixed upon the conversion of some impenitent individual.* He would address the individual with great solemnity, urging an immediate compliance with the terms of the Gospel; and as his friend accompanied him homewards, such was sometimes the pressure upon his heart, that they would seek a retired spot, and there, even in the depth of winter, kneel and plead with God for the person's salvation. His anxiety for individuals was frequently such, that he could not rest, but would leave his business to seek an interview with them, or address them by letter, or pray for them. Many of these efforts were so retired that his wife came to the knowledge of them only as he alluded to them in their private supplications to God.

"At social interviews," says the same friend, "when a number of relatives met, and God and the value of the soul seemed to be forgotten, he would sometimes beckon to me, and we would go out, seek a place of retirement, join in prayer for some perishing sinner; and then return to the company under the hallowed influence of such an exercise."

Captain T——, a few days after his death, with tears fast flowing down his cheeks, bore witness to his fidelity to souls, and added: "But for the efforts of Mr. Page and a dear Christian friend of his, my soul, to all human view, must have been lost."

Rev. M—— B—— says: "I was attending Mr. Page's school when he became a Christian; and never shall I forget how he talked to us with tears, and prayed with us. It was *then that my mind was first seriously impressed.*"

Mr. D—— N—— says, Mr. Page's faithful conversation, as they were on the way to a prayer-meeting, was the means of *tearing from him a false hope,* and bringing him at length, as he trusts, to the saving knowledge of Christ.

Another estimable friend (Mr. C—— T——) says: "His Christian character was unusually even, and unusually elevated. He deeply sympathized with those *in affliction and trials,* and was ever ready to minister to their necessities, and contribute to their comfort. But his *great object was to benefit the soul;* to bring the impenitent to Christ, and to awaken and quicken the people of God. I have often heard persons, in relating their religious exercises, say, 'Mr. Page's conversation first led me to think seriously of my soul and eternity.'

"There was an interesting little meeting" (alluded to above by the pastor) "of which I think he was the mover, in which a few brethren, residing four or five miles apart, united in secret for prayer, and which was continued for about two years. They conversed, they wept, they prayed. He encouraged them to persevere; occasionally selected particular individuals as subjects of united prayer; and sometimes would earnestly inquire, 'Is there any thing whereby we cannot be agreed in this thing? Is there any unkind feeling among us? What is it that hinders the blessing?' and this course was pursued till God appeared in the salvation of sinners.

"Many, very many, with whom he conversed and prayed, were impressed at different times, little being known of his efforts for them till their hopeful conversion. His anxiety for them was often very great. He was distressed for them. From time to time he would say to a Christian brother, 'pray for such a one;' and it seemed that he could not give over till they were brought to repentance; and sometimes almost, that he must sink unless they were converted.

"He loved those who reflected the image of Christ, and to pray, and weep, and rejoice with them. I have just met a brother, who said, Were I to recall former scenes I could tell many times when I have kneeled down alone with Brother Page to pray."

One consideration that satisfied his mind of the propriety of changing his sphere of effort, was, that he *could think of no young person within the bounds of the congregation,* (and the young he ever considered as, under God, the hope of the church,) *whom he had not seriously addressed, either personally or by letter,* on the subject of their salvation. Many of them had already united with the church, while others had become apparently insensible to the motives of the Gospel.

We have taken some pains to ascertain the subsequent history of the several individuals to whom the moving appeals inserted, or referred to above, were addressed, and the initials of many of whom are given; and though four or five have continued still far from God, and two or three, who appeared to run well for a time, have faltered in their course, and the subsequent history of several is unknown, yet upwards of *thirty* are recognized, who have either hopefully died in Christ, or still live adorning their profession of faith in him.

A reference has also been made to lists of scholars belonging to the two schools in Coventry, taught by Mr. Page; one for five and the other for two winters, being one hundred and ninety-five in all; the history of seventy of whom is unknown; and of the remaining one hundred and twenty-five, *eighty-four* are thought to have given evidence of piety, and *six* are preachers of the Gospel.

It is probable that his efforts for individuals were the means of increasing the obduracy of some, and of exciting in others a degree of personal hostility. The danger of both these results he seriously considered; and scrupulously endeavored to direct all his efforts with that kindness and discretion which should give no just occasion for either. But he came to the deliberate conclusion, that, if he would be truly faithful, such results could not be wholly avoided; and made up his mind to do what the claims of God and of perishing souls required, leaving the results with him.

To withhold the truths of the Gospel, because they may be perverted, would be to stop the mouth of every minister, and prevent the circulation of the pure word of God itself. "We," says the great apostle to the Gentiles, "are a sweet savor of Christ in them that are saved, and in them that perish. To the one we are the savor of death unto death, and to the other the savor of life unto life." Such is the fact with every form in which the Gospel can be presented, though by "an angel from heaven;" and in the mind of Him who commanded it to be "preached to every creature," it constitutes no objection, and no excuse for neglect of duty, in any one, from the preacher addressing the great congregation, to the Bible and Tract distributor, the Sabbath School teacher, and the humblest Christian who speaks a word to one of his fellow-men for Christ and eternity.

CHAPTER 7

FROM THE TIME OF HIS CONNECTION WITH THE AMERICAN
TRACT SOCIETY TO THE REVIVAL OF 1831—EMBRACING
THE PERIOD OF THE SIGNAL DISPLAYS OF DIVINE GRACE
IN THE TRACT AND BIBLE HOUSES.

We now follow our brother into a new sphere of action: a plain and
humble Christian, a stranger in a large city full of display, and dis-
sipation, and crime; and with his hands full of responsible labor for a public
institution.

Being appointed Agent of the General Depository of the American Tract
Society, formed at New York in 1825, he arrived in that city, October 10,
of that year. He had, a few months before, been spending some time in
Norwich, Conn. in drawing and engraving, and was strongly inclined to
comply with a request to locate himself there; but he felt that the opening
for usefulness in connection with the American Tract Society, was such, that
he "could not conscientiously decline it." He had visited the city; and the
responsibilities involved, with the question whether his family could live
on the compensation proposed, caused him to pass a sleepless night, till the
text, *"Trust in the Lord and do good, so shalt thou dwell in the land, and
verily thou shalt be fed,"* resolved his doubts, and he determined to follow
the indications of Providence, and commit his way to Him.

The pressure of duty, of which he speaks in the following letter, rested
upon him henceforward till his death; rendering his future correspondence
comparatively brief, and confined to the points of practical interest which
had at the moment the strongest hold on his mind.

"*New York, July* 11, 1826.

"HONORED AND DEAR PARENTS,—I can write only a few hasty lines.
My time is all so occupied, that I can devote very little to friends—far less

than I could desire, even to my dear father and mother.

"Cousin H—— P—— left us last week for Troy, on her way to Vermont. She is an interesting girl. Since she came here, I think there has been a material change in her character. She once thought that she lived in the enjoyment of religion, but grieved the Spirit, and for a long time neglected prayer. I think now there are many favorable indications in her case.

"I have lately taken the *superintendence of a Branch Sunday School,* connected with the Central Church in Broome-street; the old school to retain one hundred and fifty scholars, and mine to be increased till they are equal, and then add to both. We have two large and commodious rooms; and hope both schools, if we can get teachers, will soon embrace five hundred scholars. I don't know but I am taking too much upon me; but the request was so urgent, that I could not deny it. With Divine influence, it is a great field for usefulness.

"I heard that a Wednesday evening prayer-meeting was attended in Coventry, and that but *three* male members were present besides Rev. Mr. C——. Alas, how fallen! Is he not almost discouraged? Shall there be no 'Aarons and Hurs' to hold up his hands?

"Your affectionate son,

"H. Page"

Just before leaving his family, the young lady above alluded to, wrote him a letter, expressing her sense of the dangerous condition in which she had been living, and her need of Divine grace and strength to keep her from again falling, and adds:

"I feel, cousin H. that you have been an instrument in the hand of God of awakening me, and directing me to a throne of mercy; and could I approach it in an acceptable manner. I know you would be amply rewarded for all the anxiety you have felt on my account. I beg of you still to pray the Lord to have mercy upon me, to give me a sense of *sin*, to guard me against temptation, and to forgive and receive me."

From Troy, she again wrote him a full letter, describing her religious feelings, thanking him for his fidelity, and asking his prayers; and soon proceeded on her way to Vermont; but before arriving at the place of her destination she was called to her eternal state.

On the 15th September one of the officers of the church in Coventry wrote him, bewailing the prevalent declension in religion. "The vacancy caused by your removal," he adds, "is not filled. Many who used to lead in our prayer-meetings are removed; others have retired, and the efficient, energetic members of the church are greatly diminished; yet I hope there are some who are mourning over the desolations of Zion."

In a letter from Mr. Page to his parents, December 15, he gives the following items:

"Last evening we had the male and female children of our two Sabbath Schools arranged in the church each side of the middle aisle, filling the slips from the pulpit to the door: one hundred and thirty-four boys and nearly as many girls, with forty teachers, were present. Rev. Mr. J—— addressed them, and commanded the strictest attention.

"We have at this time a great press of business. Within a little more than a week I have sent off, for different parts of our country, not far from 1,700,000 pages of Tracts. Should each Tract be accompanied by the Divine blessing in sanctifying and saving a soul, what an amount of good would be effected!"

We cannot but feel grateful for a few such letters as the following, addressed to his beloved parents; detailing with child-like simplicity, as a means of rendering them content that he should be absent from them, some of the indications that God was blessing his efforts.

"Sabbath eve. 10 *o'clock, March* 11, 1827.

"My dear Parents,—Expecting an opportunity to send tomorrow, I improve a few moments to speak of the goodness of God to us, and of some interesting things which have recently occurred.

"O. R. K. arrived on Thursday. I hoped to hear by him, of a powerful revival of religion in Coventry, and that many of my acquaintance were subjects of it; but I am disappointed. What can be the matter? Why is not the church awake? Is any darling sin of more value than immortal souls? I will, however, give thanks, that some have been born into the kingdom of Christ. Remember me with much affection to them all.

"Besides a press of labor at the Depository, I have *my hands full of business more directly connected with the welfare of souls.*

"In the *Sabbath School* under my charge are about twenty teachers, one half of whom were, not long since, without hope. *Six* of that number, promising young men, now give evidence of piety, and the remainder, I think, are unusually serious. One of the little boys, I found today to be distressed for his sins, though the scholars in general are very careless. The school today consisted of one hundred and sixty-two boys. In the female school there have also been some conversions.

"*A Teacher's prayer-meeting* has been held weekly for both schools, and has been very solemn and interesting. At the last meeting about thirty were present. In sustaining this, considerable responsibility rests upon me.

"In the *congregation* too, a wide field for effort is open, and there are very few efficient male members of the church. About fifteen attended the last inquiry meeting; a number were deeply affected. There have been several instances of conversion besides those mentioned above.

"In the *Tract and Bible houses* we have lately had a season of uncommon interest. A work of grace commenced a few weeks since among the young women employed in the two houses in folding and stitching Bibles and Tracts, as the fruits of which we now number about *sixteen* hopeful conversions. It has been a most interesting and wonderful display of God's power and grace. On one day *seven* of them hope that they were brought from nature's darkness into the light and liberty of the Gospel. That was one of the most interesting days of my life. Twice or thrice I was sent for to pray with them, and to take the hand of those who had just been brought to bow at the Savior's feet, while, with tears streaming from their eyes, they expressed the hope that they had surrendered themselves entirely to Him. Two of these had thought that I talked too severely, and discouraged them; they now wished to thank me for the very efforts in their behalf, of which they had before complained. To see those who were brought to hope in Christ clinging around their former companions in sin, and with tears beseeching them to come at once to the Savior they had found so precious, was enough to move a heart of stone. I could say much more; but this must suffice. It was indeed the wonderful power of God. This week we design to have a general meeting for all employed in both houses, male and female, and hope God has still greater blessings in store. The meetings have hitherto been sustained chiefly by those connected with the societies, and an active Christian, who resides near.

"I say these things, that you may see that I have a field in which I may labor to good advantage—whether I enter it with all my heart, is another question.

"My love to my dear sister. Your affectionate son,

"H. PAGE"

We well remember the day above alluded to. A glow of heavenly ardor burned in our brother's countenance; and, when attempting to pursue his accustomed business, his mind seemed scarcely to know how his hands were employed. His whole soul was on fire with love to souls, and joy and exultation in the triumphs of Divine grace. "Never before," said he, "have I so sensibly felt the presence of the Spirit, or the force of those words: 'Stand still, and see the salvation of the Lord.'"

In a letter to his parents, August 21, 1827, he expresses great alarm at the *prevalence of iniquity and infidelity* in the city, and mentions that a club of infidels regularly assembled on Sabbath evening, in a spacious room, where their principles were inculcated, in every alluring and deceptive form, upon the minds of hundreds.

"Pray for us," he proceeds. "Were it not that the Lord of hosts is jealous for his own glory, we should have nothing to expect but to see the wicked triumph. *When will God's people put on the harness!*

"I have been exerting myself to have a number of theological students engaged *among the poor and destitute of the city,* during their vacations. The Central Church will employ one or two. It is believed that not far from 100,000 inhabitants of this city attend on no regular religious instruction. I ask again, pray for us. We need now forty missionaries with the zeal of Paul, to proclaim God's truth to these perishing multitudes. But no persevering, energetic means are yet adopted to obtain *any.*"

The facts concerning the infidel meetings above referred to, Mr. Page at this time carefully collected and published in the religious papers, as an incitement to Christians generally to redouble their exertions.

One of the four individuals who so long met in concert for private prayer, writes to Mr. Page, August 25, that he had just attended a prayer-meeting at his father's, where his children were present on a visit, and adds, "While pleading for them, my heart was very much enlarged; I seemed to climb up near to my heavenly Father; and calling to mind the many, O how many, precious seasons I had spent in retirement with you and my two other friends, in pouring out our supplications especially for our children, I seemed to 'travail in birth' for them, till Christ should 'be formed in them,' the hope of glory."

To this letter he replied as follows:

"*Thursday evening, N. York, Sept.* 13.

"MY DEAR BROTHER,—Your very kind and fraternal letter almost overwhelmed us. You know, my dear brother, the tender chords of a parent's heart; and the thrilling sensations produced when they are made to vibrate by the efforts and prayers of Christian friends, who *feel* for the salvation of our children. As you described the scene at my father's, and showed me my dear brethren pleading for the souls of my children, I could only weep with gratitude, that some supplications had arisen for them from those who stood near the mercy seat. You will, I trust, remember them still. You are not forgotten in some of our little praying circles.

"I was pained at your description of the prayer meeting, where no male member of the church but yourself was present. That wretched sentiment, which *releases Christians from moral obligation during harvest-time,* you know I could never away with. Give my love to all the little circle; and though we meet not again here, may we meet in heaven.

"Your affectionate friend and brother,

"H. Page"

Under date of November 4, 1827, we have a letter from Mr. J. H. then at Mobile, which presents another example of the fidelity of Mr. Page to the *members of his own household*. Mrs. H—— was then residing in the family of Mr. Page, and had written to her husband informing of his fidelity in warning, instructing and praying for her, and of the joy and peace she then had in believing in Jesus. Mr. Page had also written to confirm the joyful tidings. The deep emotions of the husband are poured out in a full sheet.

"It is impossible," he says, "to express the emotions awakened by your truly affectionate letter. My heart is so full that I scarcely know how to thank you for all your goodness to *me*, and above all for what you have done for my companion. O my dear Sir, what must be your happiness to have been the instrument in the hands of the Holy Spirit in bringing peace to the soul of our beloved A——. Her whole mind seems bent upon one theme—the love of Christ."

The following is at least another evidence of the various methods he adopted to awaken the attention of individuals to the concerns of eternity.

"Lines received, by a lady uncommonly skillful on the harp and the piano.

"Permit a stranger to express the delight with which, in the stillness of the evening, he has paused to listen to those notes, which have been so sweetly, so plaintively, or so wildly obedient to the skill of your fingers and the emotions of your soul. Pardon me if I express some of the reflections awakened in my own mind.

"'Alas,' thought I, 'those fingers which produce such thrilling emotions will soon be motionless in death. Those keys will no more tremble at their touch; those notes will be hushed to silence; and the steps of the stranger be no more arrested except by a plaintive dirge from some friend of her who sleeps in death. What then will be her state? Is her heart now prepared to sing that song which none but the redeemed can sing? Are her sins forgiven? Is Christ, the bleeding Lamb, her chief beloved? This to me is all unknown.'

"That you may be one of the performers in that grand chorus, which ascribes 'Blessing, and honor, and power to Him that sitteth upon the throne, and to the Lamb for ever and ever,' is the earnest prayer of an affectionate friend, who will probably be personally unknown to you until the judgment of the great day."

To his parents he writes, December 5: "The Lord is again doing wonders in the Bible and Tract houses. The work of grace seemed to commence
anew about three weeks since, and *more than twenty* have recently indulged
the hope that they have been born of God. We have indeed passed through
interesting scenes during this period. Last Thursday was observed by a
number of us as a day of fasting and prayer. There has been one instance of
hopeful conversion today."

An estimable and pious young lady (Miss B——) has informed the
writer, that, on becoming acquainted with Mr. Page, in 1827, he soon
inquired if she was "a professor of religion?" and again, if she "had an interest in Christ?" if she "thought it desirable?" if she "had sought to obtain
it?" if she "had renounced the world, and resolved to live for the glory of
God?" could she "give him the reason why she had not?" The impressions
made on her mind by repeated conversations were such, that she could not
rest till she found rest in Christ. "This result," she says, "I cannot but view
as in answer to fervent prayer, and in fulfillment of the promise, 'them that
honor me, I will honor.' His life was a living epistle. Often, to this day, has
the solemn question, 'Are you a professor of religion?' warned me of danger,
and summoned me to duty!'"

"New York, February 8, 1828.
"MY DEAR PARENTS—We have felt much anxiety respecting my father's
health, fearing that God may take him from us, and that it may be soon.

"I know, my dear father, that I have done many things which have
tried your feelings, and that some of them have been inconsistent with filial
duty and Christian character. These *I would beg you to forgive;* and while
you continue here, cease not to remember me before the Throne of Grace,
where we often attempt to present the wants of our dear parents, both for
time and eternity.

"I am now placed in circumstances more solemn than ever before, having been *consecrated as an officer in the church* with which I am connected,
by prayer and the laying on of hands; and if I do not have help from God,
instead of advancing, I shall only hinder his cause. The work of grace in our
congregation is gradually progressing. Thirty-five were present at the last
inquiry meeting, and several have recently indulged hope, some of whom
are teachers in my school.

"Last evening we had a meeting, which all in the Bible and Tract houses,
male and female, were invited to attend. It was very full and solemn. The
day was observed by the females in the two houses as a day of prayer, and
of special thanksgiving to God for what he has done for them the past year;

it being just one year from last evening, that the first prayer meeting was attended with them.

"Do write immediately. Your affectionate son,

"H. PAGE"

At this time, his pastor being ill, and there being an urgent call for ministerial labor, it was proposed to request Rev. Mr. C—— to leave his charge in Coventry, and labor a few weeks in the city. In endeavoring to induce the church with which he had formerly been connected to yield to this request, Mr. Page thus wrote, under date of February 28:

"I do believe, that, could the good people of Coventry come here, and see for themselves the great want of such labor as Mr. C. could bestow; could they see the thousands here going down to the grave and to perdition without instruction; and so many as there are among us solemnly affected in view of their sins, I am sure they would be willing to make any sacrifice that the great work of salvation may not be retarded. There is another world than this. Pastor and people cannot be *for ever* together on earth—death will sunder the strongest ties; and in heaven, how must it enhance the joys of the blessed, that by means of their willing sacrifices here, multitudes have been prepared to unite with them in songs for Redeeming grace. I hope the dear brethren will look at the subject with enlarged views, and pray over it, and be prepared to say, 'The will of the Lord be done.'"

The following extract from a letter to his friend A—— K——, dated April 8, shows his ardent aspirations and hopes for the rapid extension of Christ's kingdom:

"What, my dear brother, is the Lord about to do for our country and the world! What mean the interesting movements of the last half year? When I look at them, and view the hand of God in them, my blood chills, and I anticipate with astonishment the still more wonderful operations of his hand. This is indeed an eventful day. Every enterprise for Zion prospers. What would once have occupied an age, is now performed as in a day. I rejoice, my dear brother, that you have girded on the harness, and placed yourself in the ranks of those who may lead numbers on to conflict and to victory. Be not dismayed. Even one onset, if you never have strength to make another, may put to flight, in this day of God's power, an army of his enemies."

The following day he was cheered by a letter from E. F. H., who, while a teacher in his Sabbath School, had been the subject of his deep anxiety and faithful labors for his salvation; had obtained hope; united with the church; and was then a member of Middlebury College, pursuing a course preparatory to the Gospel Ministry.

"Blessed, thrice blessed," he says, "was that hour, when the Lord directed my steps to the Sabbath School, where I formed a friendship with one, which I hope will continue to all eternity. Yes, dear brother, it was *your kind voice that was the instrument*, in the hand of God, of *arresting a thoughtless wretch, and leading him to the Savior*. Henceforth you need never fear to converse with the impenitent, even with the careless worldling. I would address myself to you as my spiritual father, and still seek from you that advice and direction, which you will not refuse to give."

"New York, April 18, 1828.

"MY DEAR SISTER,—I suppose you are occupied with the cares and concerns of your family, and of this unsatisfying world; but let me ask, what are your prospects of a better state hereafter? Will any future season be more favorable to secure that good part which shall *never* be taken from you? O my sister, what will you do, should death arrive before your sins are forgiven? No parent, or husband, or brother can then help you. Prayer will cease to be availing. The Savior himself will be against you. All hope must retire for ever.

"Are you clinging to an old hope, which gives you composure, while you have *no present evidence* that your peace is made with God? If so, abandon it. Such a hope is often a prelude to a more awful, because unexpected doom.

"Your children are rising around you; and they need a *godly mother*, to pray with them, and guide them to the Friend of sinners; and they may be for ever lost for want of such a guide. Ah! could you see them standing at the bar of Christ, unconverted through an affectionate mother's neglect of their souls, how would the scene rend your heart with anguish.

"But *I will hope* better things. I will hope that they shall have a *pious mother*, and that speedily. May I not? What will you reply? God grant you may answer, '*Yes*. From this hour I surrender myself to Christ. I will be his devoted follower. I will do all in my power for the salvation of my children, and for others, until my dying day; and leave my soul with God, to dispose of me and all events according to his holy pleasure.' I have time to say no more.

"Your affectionate brother,

"H. PAGE"

On occasion of the death of the father of Mrs. Page, Mr. P. wrote a letter of consolation to the surviving sisters, in which he says:

"And now, my dear sisters, let us who remain, awake to duty. A dying world is perishing around us; lost sinners are daily entering the world of wo; and have *we* done all we can to prevent it? Have we done all we can for our impenitent relatives and friends? Have we prayed for them, and labored with them, as our consciences tell us we might have done? If there is *one impenitent individual* within the circle of our influence, whom we have not done all we can to bring to Christ, let no time be lost; let us do our duty to that soul. Let us in all respects live and act as dying sinners, who have to render to God a strict account of our stewardship. Thus doing, we may hope this solemn dispensation will be sanctified to us and others."

May 24th, he wrote a kind and filial letter to his parents, expressing his ardent desire to be with them and "smooth their way down the decline of life;" tendering them temporal aid as they might need, and endeavoring to strengthen their faith; to which he adds:

"I should like to tell you of several interesting incidents of the present week, but have no time. Give thanks to God that such a worm is used for the benefit of any soul."

His pastor having visited Europe for his health, Mr. Page, June 14, transmitted to him a narrative of what God had done for those employed in the Tract and Bible houses, hoping that it might be used as an incitement to efforts for those similarly employed for the kindred institutions in London.

In this communication, he states, that more than one hundred young women were then employed in the Tract and Bible houses, and that of these God had brought *"between fifty and sixty* hopefully into his kingdom. One of them was convicted by means of the truths which caught her eye while folding the Tract, 'Day of Judgment.'" "Many sheets of the word of God and Tracts," he says, "as they have been folded and stitched, have been moistened with the tears of the convicted sinner and the brokenhearted penitent; and thence gone out on errands of mercy to a perishing world. Every day at twelve o'clock, the females of each of the two houses devote a part of their recess, in their retired rooms, to prayer and praise; and on every Thursday evening we have a general meeting for prayer and conference, conducted by three or four brethren, the binder and printer of the two societies cordially taking part in the same."

A few days after this, he states that the seamstresses employed by Mrs. J——, residing not far distant, had also joined in the meetings in the Tract and Bible houses; that he had personally conversed with several of them, and that *five* of them had obtained hope in Christ.

At this time he was cheered with a letter from his endeared fellow-laborer in the societies' houses, (Mr. J. H. T.) who was then in the country, containing messages for their mutual charge; exhorting those who were indulging a hope to examine well its foundation, and warning those who remained impenitent to "be timely wise."

"Religion," he says, "is a personal thing; and let others do what they will, as for us, my dear brother, may we put on the whole armor of God and go forward. Although absent in body, I do not forget our friends in the societies' houses. God has done much, yet there remaineth more to be accomplished; and we, as coworkers, have much land yet to possess. May He, who has hitherto helped us, still be our guide and stay; and then, if our faith fail not, we have nothing to fear. Tell our dear sisters in Christ to persevere like good soldiers of the cross, counting nothing too dear to part with for him. Tell anxious souls to make haste and escape for their lives; submitting themselves to Christ, and owning him as their rightful sovereign and Lord. Say to careless sinners, 'How can ye escape, if ye neglect so great salvation?' 'Turn ye, turn ye, why will ye die?'"

Having a desire to learn, as far as practicable, what are the lasting results of these efforts among the females of the societies' houses, a list of *fifty-nine* who obtained hope in Christ while the efforts above referred to continued, has been placed in the hands of the writer, one of whom soon died, and all the remaining *fifty-eight* have connected themselves with evangelical churches: viz. thirteen with Protestant Episcopal churches; fourteen with Baptist churches; twenty-two with Presbyterian, five with Reformed Dutch, and four with Methodist churches. *Five* of these were among the seven mentioned March 11, 1827, as having obtained hope in one day; and *thirty-six* each gave by request a written narrative of her own religious exercises.

It is an interesting fact, that, though Mr. Page knew that those for whom he here labored were connected with different religious denominations, he neither knew nor wished to know to which most of the individuals respectively belonged.

"Sabbath evening, near ten, June 30, 1828.
(To Mrs. Page, then in Coventry.)

"We have had a precious season today. The great Master of the feast has indeed been present with us at his table. Twenty-six, I think, united with the church from the world. Among them were *five* of the teachers of my Sabbath School, and one who had been a teacher, with four or five scholars of the female school.

"I have learned this evening, that Miss J——, who has been a thoughtless girl, and was this morning at church in great distress, has come out rejoicing, which is heart-rending to some of the family who are left. They were at our meeting this evening, borne down with a sense of sin; and as I spoke to one of them, she sobbed aloud. God has been in our meeting tonight. An awful solemnity has pervaded it. Brother D—— and I held an inquiry meeting for Sabbath scholars, at a quarter before seven. More than twenty were present, and some of them deeply affected. A—— M—— seems to feel in some degree her deplorable condition; and says her mind has been impressed ever since I spoke to her a Sabbath or two since. God grant that she may flee to Christ.

"In passing out of church this P. M., I remarked to Mr. M——, that I observed he was separated from his wife at the communion season. He could hardly reply. I begged him, for his wife's sake, and for his own soul's sake, to seek an interest in Christ. He grasped my hand, and could hardly let me go. Miss. C—— appears to be wide awake in religion—a changed creature indeed.

"My dear companion, let the fire be kindled in your own heart, if it is not already kindled there; for *we* have a rising family all in their sins, and let us plead that they may not be passed by.

"I yesterday visited the sick-bed of Mrs. C——. It is sweet and refreshing to see one, who feels that she may be on the borders of the grave, so calm, so united to her Savior, and so sweetly reposing in his arms.

"This same Comforter may be yours. He is alike ready to pour his consolations into the soul of all who will confide in him, and be his willing and obedient servants. You say there is something wrong in your heart,— prostrate yourself at the foot of the cross, and let the bleeding love of a dying Savior subdue and purify it. There only can its errors be corrected.

"Your affectionate husband,

"H. PAGE"

July 15, he writes to an intimate friend: "I cannot but bless God that in his Providence he has placed me in this city, where there is so much opportunity, and so urgent a call to labor for souls. I assure you I am *never in want of something to do directly for this object.* I dare not enlarge my sphere of effort. I am already attempting so much, that it is but poorly done.

"The *Sabbath Schools* are a most interesting field for Christian exertion. I have there, as it were, a family circle, where we all feel at home. The importance of this department of effort daily increases in my view. When once we have the confidence of teachers and scholars, our influence with them, is almost unbounded. God has done great things for us—how great, eternity only can disclose."

"*New York, July* 31, 1828.
(To Mr. D. W. a friend in deep affliction.)

"MY DEAR BROTHER,—Your heart has been made to bleed; but the wound, deep as it is, has been inflicted by a kind Father. He knew, my dear brother, what you needed; and though it is most distressing, it still evinces his covenant faithfulness. Your beloved companion and our sister, has only passed over Jordan a little before us; and waits on the other shore a brief season, when all her friends, whom Jesus loves, shall be with her.

"I know not by experience the pains you feel; but I know there is a Savior, 'touched with the feeling of our infirmity,' who can and will give consolation to all who stay themselves on him. Let us, dear brother, feel that we have no abiding city here. If our 'light afflictions' wean us from the world, and make us more obedient, and faithful, and humble, we may have confidence that they shall 'work out for us a far more exceeding and eternal weight of glory.'

"The Lord, in tender mercy, is among us by his Spirit, and I trust a work is commencing which shall shake, in due time, this whole city. How blessed to labor in the service of such a Master as ours, and how animating to see sinners coming home to God!

"I hope that you will have evidence that your trials are sanctified, *by your greater activity in our Lord's service.* Don't let any, with whom you may have influence, go down to perdition without your faithful and persevering efforts to save them.

"My love to your dear children. Tell them they must be born again, or they and their dear mother will be separated for ever.

"Your affectionate and sympathizing brother,

"H. PAGE"

"*Saturday evening, N. York, Jan.* 3, 1829.

"MY DEAR FATHER AND MOTHER,—I often think of you in this excessively cold weather, and hope you are not left to suffer.

"What is the church doing in Coventry? Are they acting in full view of the approaching day of account? If they were, I think we should oftener hear of the conversion of sinners there. When, will the church awake, and make religion their *business?* This great concern must not be crowded into an obscure corner, and the world permitted to occupy the whole ground. No; religion is a business for eternity; and he that does not make it *the principal thing,* must suffer immense loss, and will perhaps ruin his soul for ever.

"Prospects with us are still encouraging. *One hundred and eight* have united with our church the past year. *Seventy-six* of them by profession. A special interest is now awakened for *heads of families,* whom we hope to see bowing to the sceptre of Immanuel.

"Your affectionate son,

"H. PAGE"

To A—— K——, who had just entered on the ministry in Ohio, he thus wrote under date of January 8: "I trust that, when this reaches you,

you will be publishing the messages of our ascended Savior to lost men. 'Lo, I am with you always,' is a blessed promise. I cannot but feel that our Missionaries at the West, if they are faithful, will gather fruit, precious and abundant. The fields are white, and it appears to me that God is about to do wonders for that portion of our land. The thousands of prayers, which have entered into the ears of the Lord of Sabaoth, must be answered. He will make his truth powerful and effectual. I think you have been sent out at a most important period of our history—that it is truly the day of enterprise for enlightening our destitute millions; and that salvation is soon to be the song of multitudes who have long lived in sin."

A letter dated, Columbus, Ohio, February 3, from F——— E——— R———, a young gentleman, who had been teacher in his Sabbath School, says: "The emotions which swell in my bosom, as I attempt to address you, are such as I cannot describe. My heart is filled with gratitude to God, that he once placed me under your particular care, and that *there I was led to embrace Christ*, as my friend and portion."

In a letter to his parents, March 6, he says: "We have now commenced presenting a Tract monthly to all the families of the city in which they are cordially received. The Tract for March is on the Sabbath, and that for April on Intemperance. This I think will prove *one of the most interesting enterprises* in which Christians of our city have ever been engaged. It will bring them to see and feel the moral wants of our neglected population; and the Lord, I trust, will prosper it."

"The Spirit of God is again moving among the young women in the Bible house. Two are under pungent convictions, who have been peculiarly hardened."

June 23, he says, "We have had an inquiry meeting this evening, which I attended alone; eight present, and some cases of deep conviction. There is now unusual solemnity among *the boys in my Sabbath school.* God grant it may not be like 'the morning cloud and early dew.'"

To his parents he wrote, February 17, 1830, mentioning an illness of about ten days. "For six hours," he says, "I was in *agonizing pain; and* obtained relief only by the most powerful medical assistance. I am confident these are chastisements I need, though I fear they have not produced the desirable effect. *I have been neglecting duty, and become cold in my religious services and affections.* O that I might live as expecting to end my pilgrimage, and render up my final account to God."

To a friend in deep affliction he writes, September 14: "You are not left *alone.* The Lord Jesus Christ has said, 'I will never leave thee nor forsake thee.' Though all earthly friends should fail and die, that blessed promise, *'I will never leave thee*, is better than all.'"

On Sabbath, October 10, he had the satisfaction of seeing his eldest son, with whom, in his deep anxiety and distress for his sins, both father and mother had some months before spent the greater part of one whole night in prayer, publicly consecrating himself to the service of Christ by uniting with his visible church.

The following letter shows that such a pleasure was soon renewed:

"New York, December 14, 1830.

"My dear Parents,—I have now the satisfaction to inform you that E——, *our only daughter, has publicly professed her faith in Christ,* and I hope she may be a humble follower of him through evil report and through good report, and be an honor to the Christian name. If she has really become a child of God, how infinitely better than all the blessings that earth can yield. *Sixteen* others united with the church last Sabbath by profession.

"My love and thanks to friends and neighbors for their kindness during my father's sickness. We are all of us, parents and children, nearing our long home; and soon, if we are the real followers of Christ, we shall be *at rest.* Let us all prepare, and look, and wait for it, that the hour of our transfer come not unawares.

"Your affectionate son,

"H. Page"

CHAPTER 8

FROM THE COMMENCEMENT OF THE REVIVAL OF 1831
TO HIS LAST SICKNESS—EMBRACING RESULTS OF HIS
SABBATH SCHOOL, HIS SUPERINTENDENCE OF CHRISTIAN
EFFORT CONNECTED WITH TRACT DISTRIBUTION, AND
THE TRANSFER OF HIS LABORS TO A NEW CHURCH.

"New York, January 24, 1831.
(To Rev. A. K., Ohio.)

M Y DEAR BROTHER,—The Lord appears now to be coming down
in all parts of this great city, to arouse his children and to awaken
sinners. Thousands of Christians here, are, I think, praying as they never
prayed before. Public general meetings commenced yesterday afternoon,
and are to be continued through the week. Conversions are occurring in
all parts of the city. Churches and ministers of different denominations
are beginning to awake. Meetings for inquiry were held in several churches
on Monday evening, and were very encouraging. Stout-hearted men are
brought to bow, as well as youth and children. We tremble lest, by our
unfaithfulness or other sins, we shall impede the work, and grieve the Spirit
of God. Churches are daily crowded to overflowing; and a most fixed and
solemn attention is given to the dispensation of the truth.

"Your affectionate brother,

"H. PAGE"

"New York, Tuesday, February 1, 1831.

"MY DEAR PARENTS,—Though brother S—— will tell you much from
us, yet I cannot forego the privilege of giving you some notice, with my
own hand, of WHAT GOD IS DOING HERE. His children are awaking—
many are giving up their former hope—thousands, I think, are wrestling
for the general descent of the Holy Spirit. Prayer meetings at daybreak are

held in various parts of the city, where Christians seem to agonize for the blessing. Ministers are seeing eye to eye. Meetings are crowded, and awfully solemn. They were held daily last week, and they commence again today. Sinners are awakened, and many have been converted. I have heard from several inquiry meetings held last evening. They were full, and there were a number of cases of hopeful conversion. The severe storm did not prevent attendance. We are expecting, my dear parents, that God is about in a signal manner to shake this whole city, and to Him shall be all the glory.

"One year ago, had we been told of what we even *now* see, we should have said, 'If God should open the windows of heaven, can such a thing be?' Two of the teachers of my Sabbath school, brothers, were hopefully converted the past week, and several of the scholars are deeply impressed.

"A case occurred last week of *special encouragement to praying parents.* At the close of the afternoon exercises, a meeting for religious inquirers was held in the Lecture-room, and a few professors, who lived at a distance, staid in the church till the evening service. Among them were two mothers, who, though strangers to each other, agreed to go to a retired pew, and spend the season in prayer. As the question arose what they should pray for, one said, 'I have a daughter who has no hope.' The other replied, 'So have I an only daughter, and she is now in the inquiry meeting, and we will pray for them.' They kneeled, and while they were still praying, one of the daughters came, found her mother, and as soon as she could do it without interrupting her, took her by the hand, saying, 'O, my mother, I hope I have found Christ to be precious.' They all knelt again in prayer, and offered their united thanksgiving to God. The other daughter was hopefully converted on the following day.[1]

"Several very interesting cases have occurred, but I cannot communicate them now. We expect God will do great things among us this week.

"Do beg my dear friends at Coventry to let all their energies be awake; for we trust the kingdom of heaven is at hand. Let them 'prepare the way' of the Lord, that no stumbling blocks hinder the conversion of sinners. My love to all who love the Lord Jesus.

"Your affectionate son,

"H. PAGE"

Mr. A—— R——, then Agent of the American Tract Society at Boston, acknowledges a letter from Mr. Page, dated February 28, of which he says:

"The facts it contained, showing the efficacy of prayer and the power of Divine grace manifested in the conversion of so many in one family, are

---

1 A note, dated March 7, says, "Both of these daughters were yesterday, as I have understood, to be united to the two churches of which their parents are members."

truly striking, and exceedingly encouraging to Christians. I read the letter in our church on Sabbath evening. This evening Rev. Mr. G.'s church will hear the same; and I intend to have extracts read in all our churches. That letter, I ardently believe, will be instrumental of good among us."

In a letter, dated, Sabbath evening, April 3, he says: "This day has been one of unusual interest in our church. Our pastor was never more direct and earnest in his appeals. He seemed to have aid from on high. Text in the morning, 'Go thy way for this time.' His object was to show that sinners feel that it depends on their own choice whether they will accept of Christ. P. M. 'Their feet shall slide in due time.' The assembly was solemn, and the appeal urgent and powerful. This evening, the meeting has also been crowded and very solemn."

It is truly a painful fact, that this is *all* that remains from the brother's pen, of his labors, prayers, and success, during by far the most signal revival of religion ever enjoyed in New York; and as the fruits of which, there was an accession to Evangelical churches of about *two thousand souls.* His whole soul was on fire from week to week. Besides the routine of his official duties, he attended the prayer-meetings at day-break; visited many individuals at intervals during the day, introducing at once the subject of religion, making a short prayer with them, and giving them the instruction he thought best adapted to their state; almost every evening he was in a religious meeting, and generally expending all the powers of his mind and heart for the eternal welfare of some individuals he there met; the spiritual welfare of his own children and household, and of more than two hundred teachers and schol- ars in his Sabbath school, pressed upon his heart; and the full measure of his powers was employed, that, while the Holy Spirit was descending, not a sheaf of the spiritual harvest should be lost. His mind and his movements were rapid. *The chain of communication from his own to other's hearts was bright.* His feelings were thrown out into a prayer meeting, or a Sabbath school, or in visiting families or individuals, almost instantaneously, as soon as his lips were opened; he accomplished very much in the space of a day; and in the ardor of his efforts, while having a spirit of prayer, and seeing the displays of divine grace, it was impossible for him coolly to sit down and calculate whether his strength of body could long endure the continual drafts made upon it. A few days hence might be the season for relaxing his endeavors; but NOW was the season of effort, and that NOW was, with him, almost perpetual.

As the warm season approached, and brought with it accumulated labors for the society he served, he found that his incessant effort had exceeded his bodily strength, and occasioned a renewed inaction of the liver, accom- panied by a slight bleeding at the lungs, which nothing but repose could restore, and which for several weeks confined him chiefly to his room.

In this state of health, he felt compelled, on May 14, to *tender his resignation as superintendent of the Sabbath school*, to the duties of which station he had consecrated his vigorous and persevering efforts for nearly five years, and with the most encouraging success.

Among the means of usefulness in this sphere, he had formed a *Sabbath School Temperance Society*, though he had no knowledge that such an experiment had then been made; and he had at length the pleasure to have enrolled the names of *thirty-two teachers*, and *one hundred and eighty* male pupils, as subscribers to the temperance pledge.

Finding that many of the boys were *profane*, he also made assiduous endeavors to correct that evil; frequently calling on all to give testimony, by rising, whether they had sworn during the week, and using all possible means to induce them to reverence the name of God. His report on this subject states, that, whereas three fourths of the boys had formerly been profane, he had reason to believe that only a few hardened individuals persisted in the sin.

The sins of *lying* and of *Sabbath-breaking* among them, he also labored perseveringly to correct; and frequently held meetings of such as were serious, at his own house, for conversation and prayer. Especially did the religious welfare of the *teachers*, many of whom, in the earlier part of his connection with the school, were not pious, engage his ardent endeavors; and during the period that he acted as superintendent, *thirty-two* male teachers hopefully embraced Christ, and united with the church, nine of whom have entered on a course preparatory to the ministry. Another teacher, (Mr. R. O. D.) whose heart was knit with his in this labor of love, is now a preacher of the Gospel, and has consecrated himself to the work of a missionary in India.

Though devoting his efforts more immediately as superintendent of the large male Sabbath school, the female school was also under his general supervision. In a communication to the female teachers at the time of his resignation, he says: "I would gratefully acknowledge the loving kindness of our God, in permitting me to be associated so long with such a band of Christ's friends; and allowing me to witness the hopeful turning to him of *from fifty to sixty, or more teachers*, connected with our two schools, and *several of the scholars*, all of whom I hope to meet at last in the great assembly of the redeemed in heaven."

As soon as he so far regained his health that he could leave the city, he repaired to Coventry; where he spent several weeks of rest from every effort beyond the degree of exercise on horseback and otherwise, which was essential to his most rapid restoration.

During this season of relaxation, he amused himself by drawing sketches of various scenes in the place of his nativity, among which he did not omit the humble dwelling where he had spent near thirty-four years of his life, and where, at the period of his death, his aged parents still resided. The sketch is a facsimile of the house, the joiner's shop and the surrounding objects.[1] After his return to New York, at the request of one who had often attended the meetings in the societies' houses, he copied it into her album; and as the claims of poetry were alike unheeded by both, he threw underneath it the following lines:

> "Here, a child, I sinned and strayed;
> "Here, the Savior disobeyed;
> "Here, I felt his chast'ning rod;
> "Here, I trust, returned to God."

In reference to his illness, he wrote to Mrs. Page: "We have great occasion to speak of the goodness of God to us. We have hardly, as yet, been called to 'run with the footmen.' Let us see to it, that we secure a divine helper to sustain us when called to 'contend with horses,' and meet the 'swellings of Jordan.'"

A letter to a relative, October 11, contains the following passage:

"Has M—— indeed done *all he can do?* Let him then fall at the feet of Jesus, and tell HIM so. Let him tell Him, that he would love Him, that he would submit to Him, that he would be sorry for his sins, that he would be an obedient child; *but he cannot.* O how unwilling the sinner is to confess all the guilt which the word of God imputes to him, and to acknowledge himself justly condemned."

In December, his eldest son, who had for five years been associated with him in labors for the Tract Society, having expressed a desire to study with a view to the ministry, he placed him in the Manual Labor Department of an Academy in Massachusetts; accompanying his farewell with the following paternal counsel:

"New York, December, 1831.

"MY DEAR SON,—As you have now entered on a very important period of life, and are about to be separated from home, you will gratefully receive a few hints from your affectionate father.

"Let it be your first object (for without this all other acquirements will be in vain) to be a humble, holy, consistent Christian, till death shall

---

1 See the frontispiece, page 2.

separate you from all earthly scenes and responsibilities.

"By uniform kindness and propriety of deportment, endeavor to merit the love and respect of all. Never indulge a spirit of retaliation. Yield a cheerful obedience to the requisitions of your instructors; join no combinations for resisting authority; and mingle with no companions whose reputation you would not wish to share.

"Be careful of your health, if you would accomplish any thing of moment for yourself or the world; govern your appetite; have regular hours for sleep and exercise. Do not place too much confidence in a vigorous constitution; it will not long be trifled with, with impunity.

"The Bible should be your daily text-book; and according to the request of your mother, endeavor also to read every day a portion of Baxter's Saints' Rest, or some kindred author, and to form your life by such models. If your studies will permit, always have some useful book in a regular course of reading.

"In your religious duties, as in every thing else, system will be necessary. Let nothing prevent your holding communion with God, on your knees in your closet, at least twice every day. *Meditate* there, as well as read and pray. Daily prayer with your roommate should be maintained, if agreeable to him; but let not this be made a substitute for closet prayer. Unite yourself with a select circle for social prayer and the cultivation of devotional feelings, and take part in the exercises when requested. In hearing preaching, guard against a spirit of criticism. Let the Sabbath be to you a holy day. Remember it as God would have you.

"Keep constantly in mind, that the object of your education is to prepare you to do the greatest possible good; and *try to be useful every day.* Think much of Christ, and commit your all to him. Go on, my son; aim to be eminently holy and eminently useful; and may the Holy Spirit guide and cheer and bless you.

"Make confidants of your parents. None will sympathize with you like them. They will soon sleep in the dust. While they live, give them the consolation to believe that your heart is set on being and doing good; and should you survive them, act and feel as you know they would have desired, and as God will approve. And when we all meet at the great day, may they and the universe see that you have not lived in vain.

"Your AFFECTIONATE FATHER"

Having resigned the superintendence of the Sabbath school, he labored, as he regained his health, to promote its interests by visiting to obtain scholars; and about the beginning of the year 1832, commenced instructing a *Female Bible Class;* and also yielded to earnest solicitations by assuming the *superintendence of the system of Christian effort in connection with Tract distribution in the Fourteenth Ward,* containing not far from three thousand families, in which work he had the cooperation of *thirty-six* male and female distributors or Tract Missionaries.

They had not long pursued this enterprise, when he clearly saw that, as little more was done than to present a Tract monthly to each family, there was *no such direct, faithful, personal and persevering effort and wrestling prayer for particular individuals,* as duty to God and the souls of men demanded. At the meeting of his fellow-laborers in January, he therefore laid the subject solemnly and earnestly before them, depicting the spiritual wants of the ward; the condition of hundreds of families who absented themselves from the stated means of grace, and who, unless reached by their efforts, would probably never have the offers of salvation pressed on their attention. He urged their obligations to God and the souls of the perishing; and then inquired of each distributor, whether there were not in his district, some one or more individuals, for whom he felt that there was special encouragement to labor, and to whose salvation he would direct his own devoted efforts and prayers, till he should have evidence of conversion, or that the door of useful access was closed. It was made a subject of prayer and heart-searching with each distributor, till one fixed his mind on one individual, another on two, and another on three or more, and by the thirty-six distributors eighty-eight individuals were thus selected as special objects of their prayers and affectionate endeavors for their salvation.

This gave them, as will be readily conceived, a new impulse in their work. They saw a distinct object before them, important as eternity, and yet one in which they could do nothing without the marvellous displays of Divine grace. They went to the throne of mercy. They went to the objects of their affectionate solicitude, and their mouths were filled with arguments. Access was easy. The Spirit of God seemed to have gone before them, and to go with them.

His duties as Superintendent did not prevent him from taking a portion of this work regularly upon himself. An instance of the encouragement he met, is recorded in the following letter.

"New York, June 21, 1832.

(To Mrs. Page.)

"Last evening I closed up our efforts in the Tract distribution for this month, and gave in my report. A few hours before the meeting, I found that a district of seventy-eight families had not been supplied; and to complete the distribution for the ward, undertook to supply it myself. I found several, whose minds were very tender, and on whom the truth seemed to make a deep impression. A *young man and his wife* listened with fixed and trembling attention, as I conversed with them on the subject of their own personal salvation. Two pious females residing in the house, soon joined the little circle, and we all knelt and endeavored to commit their case to Him who is able and willing to save. It was a solemn season, and our Divine Redeemer seemed to manifest his special presence.

"This morning I *called on them again.* I found both of them apparently trusting in the Savior. They hoped they had surrendered themselves to Him on the preceding evening. They had opened to each other freely the feelings of their hearts; and had that morning erected the family altar, and were now determined to live together as fellow-heirs of the grace of life.

"The husband of the woman who was thought last month to give evidence of conversion, is now also rejoicing with her, and they appear to be walking together in wisdom's paths.

"Your very affectionate husband,

"H. Page"

During the prevalence of CHOLERA in the city, in the summer of 1832, which at one period removed more than one hundred souls daily to eternity, we find Mr. Page, not merely confiding himself and family to the care of Providence, but *laboring to improve the tenderness and concern existing in many for their eternal good.*

"An unusual solemnity and readiness for religious conversation," he says, "has prevailed; and not a few, while the pestilence has been raging around them, have been deeply affected in view of their condition as sinners. Most Christians, who have remained in the city, have exhibited a delightful trust in Christ as their all-sufficient refuge. Frequent occasions have offered, and been improved, for faithful conversation and prayer with those who were not accustomed to pray; and I cannot but hope that the efforts of this season will result in the salvation of some precious souls. The Tract on Cholera has been distributed throughout the city, and almost universally received with thankfulness."

A memorandum bearing date February 7, 1833, contains the names of *fifty-nine* individuals obtained by Mr. Page from the square in which he lived, as subscribers to the *temperance pledge.*

An illness of some weeks occasioned the two following communications:

"New York, February 18, 1833.
(To the Tract Missionaries of the Fourteenth Ward.)

"MY DEAR FRIENDS AND FELLOW-LABORERS,—For several weeks

unforeseen Providences have prevented my cooperating with you as fully as I had intended; and I much regret that I am unable to meet you this evening. As I have not the satisfaction of seeing you all at our regular meetings, I had *determined to visit you at your own places of abode*, that we might quicken and encourage each other, and unite in imploring the blessing of God on our great and responsible work; but hitherto the Lord has prevented me.

"Now, my dear friends, as you value the immortal soul, and the favor of our Divine Leader, I would urge upon every one of you to enter on your duties with new zeal, new hopes, and new confidence in God. Endeavor to fix in your mind what it is to live for ever in heaven, or in hell. How many, who are living in utter neglect of God and are reached by no other means of grace, must be left to perish, if you are not faithful to them! How many, if you do your duty, may you meet at last on Mount Zion, who shall bless God for ever, that you found them, when lost and wandering from Him.

"Fix it in your mind that you must not be satisfied, unless, through your agency, sinners are brought to repentance; nor rest, till you see each of your districts as a well-watered garden, and the reviving and saving influences of God's Spirit operating in every family. I know that in some districts there are many things discouraging; but you must adopt the language of Paul: 'I can do *all* things, through Christ which strengthened me.'

"I do not think it Christian wisdom to expend all our strength on the darkest part of our respective fields; there is soil which we may cultivate with the fairest prospect of success; and while each of us has so large a field, let us labor *principally where there is the greatest encouragement, and there be faithful and persevering.*

"As all our strength comes from God, I would propose that, in our morning and evening devotions every day for one week, we pray in concert for the outpouring of the Spirit on the families of the Fourteenth Ward; and I wish you would express your determination on this subject by a vote at your meeting.

"The Lord be with you, my dear friends, in all your labors, and give you many souls as your hire. Remember your superintendent, that he may be fitted for his work, have bodily strength, and be endued with wisdom from above.

"Your affectionate fellow-laborer,

"H. PAGE"

"*Sabbath, March* 8, 1833.
"TO THE FEMALE BIBLE CLASS.—My dear Friends,—This is the fourth Sabbath that, in the providence of God, I have been deprived of

the privilege of meeting you; but I have not forgotten you, and I trust you remember some of those things to which your attention was called while I was with you.

"In looking over my list of members, I find that *ten* of your number, as far as I know, are still in the dark way to eternal death; having none of the hopes and consolations of the Gospel, and no title to the kingdom of heaven.

"The object of this note is especially to urge you, in view of the alarming progress you have already made in sin, and of the dreadful end of all the ungodly, *this day* deliberately to make up your minds that henceforth you 'will serve the Lord.' Be blind and deaf to all the attractions, frowns, or reproaches of a gay and deceitful world; and resolutely set your faces toward heaven.

"My friends, you must not deny me—*me*, did I say? you must not deny Christ, who came 'to seek and to save' such lost sinners as you and I. He entreats you, he bids you forsake all and follow him.

"Here, my friends, though I cannot speak to you face to face, are the feelings of my heart. When we next meet, whether in this or another world, let me rejoice with you as having chosen that good part which shall never be taken from you.

"Your affectionate friend,

"H. PAGE"

"New York, March 13, 1833.

"MY DEAR PARENTS,—I am pained to hear by Mr. G. that you are so feeble, and that life seems so fast wasting away. As I may not have another opportunity of addressing you both this side the grave, I would inquire how the dark valley appears as you approach it.

"How does my dear mother feel under the distressing pains of her disease? Can she patiently and submissively say, 'It is the Lord, let him do what seemeth him good?' Is she comforted with the reflection, that he 'doth not afflict willingly, nor grieve the children of men?' Can she lean on that almighty arm which sustains all God's children in the last conflict? Many, while enduring intense suffering of body, and about to take their departure, have found that

'Jesus can make a dying bed
'Feel soft as downy pillows are.'

In his hands, my dear mother, I leave you; and though I may not again speak to you face to face here, I hope that after a little while we shall meet where pain and sorrow and sin are known no more for ever.

"And now, my dear father, as flesh and heart fail, I trust God is 'the strength of your heart;' and that your hope in Him, through Christ, is steadfast. I know that to the impenitent sinner the near approach of death and eternity is an unwelcome theme; but not so to the saint. It is his delight to think and speak about HOME—that home, which Christ has gone to prepare; and though you and my dear mother may have almost finished your journey here, I hope neither of you regret that its end is so near; but that you can wait calmly and patiently till your change come, and then commit yourselves to Him who will safely bear you through the billows of death.

"It is trying to me, that I cannot be with you; but at present it is impracticable. I have been for some weeks confined at home by impaired health. The Lord has been gently correcting us. C—— has had a violent attack of fever, and sister P—— has left us, we trust, for a better world. But I feel assured that God has sent these chastisements in mercy, and hope they will bring us all nearer to himself. The family send love, and may we all meet at last in the kingdom of our Redeemer.

"Your affectionate son,

"HARLAN PAGE"

"*New York, March* 18, 1833.

"MY DEAR SON,—I have been able to be at the Tract house but two days since early in February. My complaint commenced with chills, fever and cough, occasioned by a congested state of the liver; but by copious bleeding and other remedies the cough is removed, and I am now nearly restored.

"I beseech you, my dear son, to remember, that you live in a day when all God's children must harness themselves for the great work of the Lord. Let no delusive claims of earth gain a hold upon your affections. Go continually, as a humble, penitent sinner, to Christ, and live for God and eternity.

"The state of things in our church is more than commonly interesting. Nearly fifty attended the inquiry meeting last evening.

"Your affectionate father,

"H. PAGE"

May 30, he says: "W—— F—— departed this life yesterday, and his brother G—— is almost gone. Their tender-hearted father said to me, that he had rather bury them both in a day, and have all his anticipations of their speedily entering the ministry cut off, than to see one of them twenty-four years of age in health but impenitent."

During the remainder of the spring, and the season of anniversaries, he was constantly pressed with business at the Depository; and early in the summer made a short visit to his parents for the last time.

August 9, he says, "I do hope that some spiritual life may be restored to the Christians of our church and city. I think there are some faint indications of pulsation with a few, though hardly perceptible. Sometimes I think I have evidence of the presence of God; but alas, it is so indistinct that I hardly dare believe it to be true."

Again he says: "We have had an interesting church prayer-meeting this evening spent in conversing with the members. We have sadly declined, and some are beginning to feel it.

"I am now so pressed with business on all sides, that I can hardly find time to write even a few lines."

In December, he says, "Those engaged in Tract labors throughout the city have just observed a day of fasting and prayer. The meetings were full and solemn, morning and afternoon; and in the evening a sermon was preached from, 'Ye are the salt of the earth,' showing that every Christian should make his influence *individually and directly felt for the salvation of those around him.* We have commenced meetings again in the bindery of the Bible house. On Friday evening about eighty were present, and a deep solemnity was apparent."

"Saturday evening, January 25, 1834.

"MY DEAR PARENTS,—The Lord has in great kindness thus far preserved our health the present winter, for which I know we are not sufficiently thankful. There is an uncommon interest in religion in several of the churches, in some of which it is hoped from thirty to sixty have been converted to God.

"Monday morning, 27th. Since the above date, we have passed through scenes which will never be effaced from my memory. On Saturday evening, C—— and A—— returned from meeting about nine. Nothing was said, and all were seated, when A—— broke the silence by sobbing in great distress for her soul. The Holy Spirit had set her sins in order before her, and she was troubled. We all felt that this invisible and blessed Agent was present; and only C. could restrain his tears. I asked the sobbing child what was the cause of her distress. She replied, that she was a great sinner against God. I endeavored to present Christ clearly to her mind as the Savior of sinners, and show her her duty to humble herself at his feet, and yield herself without delay wholly to Him. We all knelt and committed her case to God with strong crying and tears. It was hard to cease pleading till we had evidence that she had surrendered herself to Christ. But there seemed a reluctance to yield up all for him. After further conversation and prayer, Mrs. Page and myself retired to our chamber, where we again plead for her and the other children before God, and committed ourselves to rest.

"About one o'clock, A—— came to our bed-side saying: 'I hope I have given my heart to Christ. I have been a very naughty girl. Do forgive me. I will love you now, and try to do as you wish to have me.'

"On Sabbath morning, W—— was alarmed in view of his sins. When he came from church at noon, he was overwhelmed. The family were all in tears. We all fell on our knees and spent an hour in prayer, W—— still sobbing and begging for mercy.

"These scenes affected C——. The most solemn attention to the concerns of their souls was manifested by him and W—— at the meetings in the afternoon and evening, and during the remainder of the day; and now both are hoping in Christ, and seem resolved to serve him alone. I hope for them with trembling. Time will determine whether the work is genuine. God grant that they may not be deceived. It will be wonderful grace indeed, if these three children, from eleven to twelve years old, have all been born again; but it is such grace as God in Christ can bestow. My dear parents, pray that the work of grace in them, and in all of us, may be such as shall stand the test of the final day.

"Your affectionate son,

"H. PAGE"

About this time an urgent application was made to him to unite in forming and sustaining the Brainerd Church in a very destitute part of the city. He felt the force of the request; for he had well considered the moral desolations of the city, and prayed and wept over them. To his mind no duty was clearer or more important, than that members of the older churches, filled to a great extent with professors of religion, should separate, as fields of usefulness open, and go out to form new circles of religious influence. And if it was the duty of some, and others did not enlist in the enterprise, why should he not go himself? True, his health was already enfeebled, and the additional labor might crush him; but he was not accustomed to spare himself, and made the sacrifice, as he believed, at the call of duty.

This transfer of his field of labor made it necessary that he should resign the superintendence of the Tract distribution in the fourteenth ward, which he did on the 12th of February; "having felt," as he said, *more and more fully convinced of the completeness of the* PLAN *of the Tract Mission, if but faithfully carried out by praying, self-denying and devoted Christians."*

In a scrap, which he seems to have prepared as a memorandum for an address to Tract distributors or missionaries, perhaps on their day of fasting and prayer in December, 1833, the following facts appear:

From March, 1829, to January, 1832, only *four* cases of conversion were reported from the fourteenth ward, three of which were by a blessing on the reading of Tracts. Little more was done than to present them from door to door; spiritual life was wanting; and the laborers were becoming disheartened.

Of the eighty-eight individuals for whose salvation the distributors, in January, 1832, resolved steadfastly to pray and labor, more than thirty were reported in February, as at least in some degree anxious for their souls; and *three* of the number as rejoicing in God; in March, *four;* in April, *six;* in May, *three;* in June, *six;* and *twelve* in the subsequent months; making in all *thirty-four* hopeful conversions from that ward within the year 1832. Of this number three or four were awakened by reading the Tracts, and others apparently by means of the prayers and exhortations of the distributors. Many of the poor and afflicted people of God, forsaken by the world, had been found and comforted; some backsliders reclaimed; and the Gospel message delivered to numbers who continued to disregard it. Many interesting instances of the blessing of God on these efforts are alluded to in the memorandum; and it is stated, that almost all of them are the cases of individuals who were *scarcely reached by any other means of grace.*

The separation from the church with which he had been for eight years so happily and usefully connected, was indeed trying; but he went to the new field of labor with the prayers and kindest wishes and sympathies of his brethren.

"All the time he was with us," says the pastor, "he was a man of kind and peaceful spirit; always grieved at dissension in the churches, and laboring to promote a spirit of love.

"He was always *prompt in action.* What he undertook, we knew would be done, and well done; and he was ready to any work to which the great Master called him—not shrinking from self-denial, nor asking to be excused. In our meetings of religious inquiry, he was a safe and faithful laborer. Often would he seem to fix his heart intensely on the salvation of some individual; and as he saw the prospect of good, would labor with him till the hour was gone, and then accompany him to his home, still toiling to remove obstacles from the mind and bring him to accept of Christ.

"Many souls here owe their salvation, under God, to his faithful and persevering labors:—in the prayer-meeting; in the Sabbath school; in the Bible class; and especially to his personal conversation and guidance in the Christian course. His eye was single. He had one definite object before him: it was not fame, or family, or ease, or pleasure—but *to honor Christ in the salvation of men.* This singleness of purpose made him skillful and prompt in adopting means, and was the grand secret of his success.

"He left us to go to a new and unbroken field, where the toil of gathering a church was all to be borne anew; but he felt that he was consecrated, not to one particular church, but *to Christ;* and must go, and that cheerfully, at his bidding. With four such Aarons and Hurs to hold up his hands and cooperate with him, any faithful and qualified minister would be strong, under the blessing of God, for building up a new church."

As a means of furthering the new enterprise, Mr. Page again assumed the responsibilities of *Superintendent of the Sabbath school;* and put forth his devoted energies to bring the Gospel, by all practical means, to bear effectually on the surrounding population, old and young. His labors for the Tract Society were undiminished; and it was scarcely to be expected, that the constant pressure of his varied and ceaseless efforts, and the exhausting excitement of mind continually connected with them, should not bring back that derangement of the vital organs from which he had repeatedly suffered. Under date of March 25, he thus writes to his parents:

"These tabernacles of clay are wearing down, and will soon be demolished. How little should we depend upon them. If we are God's children, we have in prospect a more glorious body, where all is filled with the fullness of God. Let us look much to it, and patiently wait for it."

His strength was sustained till the results of the year in his department were prepared for the Annual Report, and the immediate pressure of the anniversary season had subsided, when he found himself exhausted; was obliged to remit his exertions; and at the advice of his physician, spent several days at Saratoga Springs, but with no improvement to his health. He returned to the city, and gradually declined till about the first of August, when it became apparent to himself and others, that his earthly labors, except from his dying bed, were closed.

A brief letter to his son, June 4th, concludes thus:

"Now I have done. Let no good resolutions be forgotten, or neglected. Remember—remember—duty—God—Christ—Judgment—Heaven—Hell.

"Your affectionate father,

"H. PAGE"

To his daughter, he wrote from Troy, June 23, on his return from the Springs: "I trust I had some special consolation last evening, in committing myself, my family, and all our concerns, into the hands of that Redeemer whose long suffering and mercy are without measure. He is doing with us what is infinitely best; and we should not desire him to change his mode of discipline in any of its details."

Two days later he writes: "I have for some time been depressed in body and spirit; have felt many anxieties and solicitudes, and had but little communion with God. I think, however, that within a few days I have had a satisfaction in resigning all my concerns to the disposal of Him, who, I am confident will pursue the best possible course of discipline, though often demanding strong faith, when the reasons of his dispensations are so entirely concealed. In order to be ripened for heaven, I need *a great deal* of purification by the Holy Spirit."

Of his labors in connection with the Brainerd Church, the young clergyman who commenced religious worship there, says: "His influence, while the Lord continued him with us, was excellent. He was *always* engaged—*always* spiritual. His zeal seemed to suffer no declension: it savored of the closet, of self-communion, of heaven. He had a wonderful tact in conducting our prayer-meetings and making them interesting: always diversified, and yet always solemn. His remarks, though simple, were never commonplace. The *point* and *spirit* of them appeared to have been premeditated, and they were generally well adapted to the character and condition of those present. In superintending the Sabbath school, he would in a remarkable degree fix the attention of the children. He had also a happy talent for addressing *strangers* on the subject of personal religion; and after our meetings would almost always single out some individual, and engage in close personal conversation. Several persons were in this way brought under conviction of sin, and some will have reason to bless God to eternity for his persevering faithfulness. His loss we feel deeply. He loved those with whom he had here been laboring, and prayed for us on his dying bed. Our members were very much attached to him, and constantly and fervently prayed that his life might be spared, could it be consistent with the Divine will."

The last item of business to which he gave the least attention, was to look at the annexed sketch of one of the scenes of the labors of David Brainerd. He had visited the spot, and drawn the sketch, and Dr. A———, having engraved it on wood, called to present it, and see if it had his approbation.

"I will look at it, but I have done with every thing here."

"You can cast your eye upon it now, and look at it again perhaps when you are stronger."

"No; I shall never look at it again. My work here is *all done.*"

VIEW OF THE CREEK AND VILLAGE OF CROSSWICKS, NEW JERSEY, JULY, 1833.

CHAPTER 9

PROMINENT CHARACTERISTICS OF HIS EFFORTS FOR THE
SALVATION OF MEN.

It may not be unimportant to bring together some of the *characteristics of his efforts to honor Christ in the salvation of individuals*, as illustrated in the preceding history.

It was *the burden of his heart, and the purpose of his life*. When engaged in his usual business, the religious welfare of persons with whose state he had become acquainted, was generally pressing on his mind; and it is now known, that for several years before he died he almost always had by him a *memorandum of the names and residence of a few individuals* with whom he was to converse. On these he would call, as he went to and from his office, or religious meetings; and *if no names were on this list*, he felt that he was doing little good. He also uniformly had in his hat more or less awakening tracts, that he might present as he should judge them adapted to the state of those he met. Not unfrequently he would seize a few moments from his usual occupation, to go out and address some individual; and when the business of the day was closed, he hastened to some meeting or other religious engagement for the evening. It is believed that an entire month has frequently elapsed, during which he did not sit down for an hour, even in the bosom of his own family, to relax his mind, or rest. Every evidence of good accomplished gave him new joy; and every opening for usefulness added a new impulse to his efforts. He felt that, under God, the eternal joy or wo of immortal souls depended on his fidelity. Each evening and each hour brought its duties, which he felt could not be neglected or postponed. The *present duty* was still before him; and though "faint," he was still "pursuing." His labors on the Sabbath were not less exhausting than on other days; and he doubtless thus failed of obtaining that "compensation for toil," which the animal constitution requires, and which is essential to a long life.

When urged, at the close of a day of fatigue, to spare himself and spend the evening at home, he would say, "Don't attempt to persuade me away from duty. I have motive enough within myself to tempt me to enjoy repose with my family; but that will not save souls." A little previous to his last sickness, as he returned from church coughing, he was asked if he had not spoken too much in the Sabbath school; "perhaps I have," he replied; "but how could I help it, when all eyes were fixed, and the children seemed to devour every word I said?"

It was not uncommon, at different periods of his life, for him in sleep to imagine himself addressing the impenitent; and to wake in a high state of excitement and in tears, occasioned by the deep sympathy he felt for their perishing condition. It is also known, that, when he saw no manifestations of the outpouring of the Holy Spirit, he would be, at times, in deep distress; would wrestle more abundantly in prayer, renew his efforts to arouse Christians to duty and awaken the impenitent; and more or less conversions were almost always the result.

In short, it was not the great object of his spiritual life, *himself to be happy in religion;* but rather by persevering labors and holy self-denial— like the Apostle who testified that he *died daily*—to glorify God in winning souls to him. He ardently desired to devote the whole undivided efforts of his life to this work, and nothing but the duty of providing for the support of his family prevented it.

He had the most clear view of the *necessity to every man of being born again.* As soon as an individual came into his presence, it seemed to be the first question of his mind, "Is this a friend or an enemy of God?" The next thing was, if impenitent, to do something for his conversion; or if a Christian, to encourage him in duty. Whatever else he saw in an individual, he felt that it availed him nothing unless he had received Christ to his heart by a living faith. This he felt and urged to be the sinner's first, great, and only duty in which he could be acceptable to God. This was exemplified at a meeting of his Sabbath school teachers, when he called on each to know whether he thought he had a well grounded hope in Christ, or not; and recorded their several replies. Among them was an amiable young merchant, whom he highly respected, and who seemed not far from the kingdom of God.

"Have you a hope?" he tenderly inquired.

"No, Sir," was the reply.

"Then I'm to put down your name as having no hope?"

"Yes, Sir."

"Well, I write down your name as having no hope."

The young man pondered on this decision and record of his spiritual state; was troubled, and soon came to our brother, saying, "I told you to put me down as having no hope; but I can't say that." He is now a member of the church, and a decided supporter of all her institutions.

He *brought his efforts to bear upon individuals, and followed up impressions made*. All the triumphs of the Gospel, he knew, consist in the conversion and sanctification of *individuals;* and he was not satisfied with merely praying and contributing for the salvation of the world as a whole; or having a general impression made on the minds of a congregation. His intense desire was that *individuals* should be turned from sin to God. Not unfrequently he would observe in the congregation a person unknown to him, who seemed to give solemn attention to divine truth; ascertain who he was, and seek a personal interview; and IN ALL CASES, if he left an individual today in an interesting state of mind, he would endeavor to see him again tomorrow; and follow up the impression at brief intervals, till there was no longer encouragement, or he had evidence of true conversion.

He had *a clear sense of obligation*, both in the sinner to repent, and in the Christian to devote all his powers to God. He felt, and labored to make others feel, that if any one neglected duty, the guilt was all his own; that God was ever ready to receive the returning prodigal; and that if any with-held their hearts, or aught they possessed from him, in the day of judgment they would be speechless. This sense of obligation he urged with unabating fervor. His heart was intent that it should be *felt*, and *immediately carried out* in an entire consecration to God.

"Brother," said he to a lovely Christian who watched with him, "when you meet impenitent sinners, don't merely say calmly: 'Friend, you are in danger;' but approach them with a holy violence, and labor to 'pull them out of the fire.' They *are* going to perdition. There *is* a heaven and a hell."

As a brother from Boston to whom several of his letters were addressed, had called for a few moments, and was about taking leave, he asked the dying man if he had any particular thought on his mind to express as he bade him farewell. "Ah, I can say nothing," he replied, "but what has been repeated over and over; but could I raise my voice to reach a congregation of sinners, I would tell them 'their feet shall slide in due time'—they *'shall slide'*—there is no escape but by believing in Christ."

He not only endeavored to alarm impenitent men, but to *bring them to a decision* that they will be the Lord's.

While in his native place, he was absent one evening till so late an hour, that his wife remonstrated with him for unreasonably tasking his own health, and separating himself from home. "I have spent this time," said he, "in trying to persuade your poor impenitent brother to give his heart to Christ." That impenitent brother was soon brought to accept of mercy; pursued a course of theological study, and is now serving God in the ministry.

On another occasion, while residing in the city of New York, he had gone to a religious meeting, and returned late in the evening, when he was reminded of the danger that his protracted efforts might be more than he could ultimately sustain. "I have been standing this hour," was his reply, "at the corner of the street, laboring with Mr. H——, (one of the teachers of his Sabbath school,) and trying to persuade him to submit to God." Within a few hours the young man found peace; soon resumed his studies which he had been pursuing for other ends; and he is now a devoted minister of Christ, gathering a flourishing church in one of the principal cities of the West. A letter from this young clergyman, received as these sheets were going to press, thus confirms this brief statement.

"The name of brother Page will ever be associated in my mind with all that is worthy of imitation in the Christian character. By the persuasions of an acquaintance, I was induced to engage as teacher in his Sabbath school; and though I was then destitute of faith, he welcomed me, and won my confidence and love. Very soon he began to address me with the utmost apparent tenderness and anxiety in reference to my own salvation. His words sunk deep into my heart. They were strange words; for though I had lived among professors of religion, he was *the first who for nine or ten years had taken me by the hand, and kindly asked, 'Are you a Christian?'* 'Do you *intend* to be a Christian?' 'Why not *now?'* Each succeeding Sabbath brought him to me with anxious inquiries after my soul's health. On the third or fourth Sabbath, he gave me the Tract 'Way to be Saved,' which deepened my impressions. At his request, I also attended a teacher's prayer meeting conducted by him, where my soul was bowed down and groaned under the load of my guilt. At the close of the meeting, Mr. Page took my arm as we proceeded on our way to our respective homes, and urged upon me the duty and privilege of an immediate surrender of my heart to Christ. As we were about to part, he held my hand, and at the corner of the street, in a wintry night, stood pleading with me to repent of sin and submit to God. I returned to my home, and for the first time in many years bowed my knees in my chamber before God; and entered into a solemn covenant to serve him henceforth in and through the Gospel of his Son. God was pleased, I trust, by his Holy Spirit, to seal my vows. If I have since had any Christian joy, or done any thing to advance the cause of Christ, it is to be attributed to the Divine blessing on the faithfulness of brother Page."

He *expected success from God, through the blessing of the Holy Spirit in answer to prayer.* He felt that humble, self-denying effort, made in God's strength, *he would own and bless;* but that for this he would be "inquired of" by his people. HE LOVED PRAYER. Besides prayers at social meetings, with the families and individuals he visited; and on special occasions, frequently recurring, he, regularly, not only conducted family worship, accompanied by singing, but every morning and evening prayed with his companion as they retired and rose, and also poured out his heart to God alone in the closet. For the latter duty, when in his native place, he often retired to a consecrated spot in a grove near his father's house. If one of the household were about to take a journey, the family assembled and commended each other to God, which was frequently done on other occasions of special interest.

His prayers were usually short and fervent, and confined mainly to those topics which pressed with special force upon his mind. At all times, prayer seemed to be a privilege, and the throne of grace a resting-place, and a solace to his heart. There is no doubt that it was by continual and fervent prayer, that he imbibed that glowing sense of eternal things, that love to souls, and that heavenly unction, which were at once the spring of his fidelity, and, under God, the ground of his success.

So anxious was he that there should be more prayer in the churches; and such were his hopes, that, if the duty were properly presented, it would be felt and practiced, that he united with a brother whose means were as limited as his own, in paying fifty dollars as a premium for a tract on prayer—himself drawing out minutely various hints to guide those who might write; and it was by this means that the excellent Tract, (No. 271,) on the obligations, nature, benefits, and occasions of prayer, was procured.

In his mind there was no jarring conflict between *perfect obligation* on the part of man, and *perfect dependence* in his relations to God. He knew both were revealed, momentous, eternal truths; and left all embarrassing questions of their consistency to be settled by God himself. It was enough, to hear God speak, and to obey. He prayed as if all the efficiency and praise were God's, and labored as if duty were all his own. His sense of dependence threw him on his knees, and his sense of duty summoned him to effort; and prayer and effort, and effort and prayer were the business of his life. Blessed day to the church, when this endless source of contention and controversy shall thus be settled in every Christian's heart!

He was *uniform and unwearied.* I know not who has made or heard the charge of inconsistency in his Christian character. Those who knew him best, best knew how supreme in his heart was the business of glorifying God in the salvation of men. I have well considered the assertion when I say, that, during nine years in which we were associated in labors, I do not know that I ever passed an interview with him long enough to have any interchange of thought and feeling, in which I did not receive from him an impulse heavenward—an impulse onward in duty to God and the souls of men. No assembly, even of professed Christians, from which *the spirituality of religion was excluded,* whether met for social enjoyment, or in furtherance of some benevolent design, received his countenance; nor was he satisfied with what too justly seemed the strange anomaly of excluding Christ from the hours of social intercourse, and then, as it were atoning for the sin, by closing the interview with prayer.

The only remaining particular which it seems important now to mention, is his FRUITFULNESS IN DEVISING EXPEDIENTS FOR DOING GOOD. Of this point the history of his life is but an exemplification.

As the father of a family, he labored for the spiritual welfare of all his household, especially for the early conversion of his children. Of thirteen individuals, who resided in his family at different times in the city of New York, twelve became deeply anxious for their salvation. One of these was a Roman Catholic, whose attention to family worship was forbidden by her priest; one, who was hopefully reclaimed from her backsliding, has since died; and six others gave, and, so far as known, still give evidence of saving conversion to God. Of his fidelity to his children, the testimony contained in the following expression of filial gratitude from his son, in transmitting, by request, the letters he had received from his father, will be excused.

"In reviewing the letters I received from my father," he says, "I see every where an expression of the tenderest solicitude both for my temporal and eternal welfare; and O for some of that ardent desire for the salvation of souls to bear me forward in duty, which impelled him onward, till he ceased his toils on earth, and entered on his rest in heaven.

"I cannot refrain from bearing testimony to my father's fidelity to my own soul. Well do I remember his endeavors in my early childhood to lead me to the Savior—his prayers—his entreaties—and the anxiety with which he followed me year after year, while under the paternal roof and when away, till he could speak to me no more. His kind voice I shall no longer hear. His affectionate smile of approval, or tears shed over my waywardness, I shall no more see. His kind intercourse with the members of his family, we shall no more share. He will no more call us around the hallowed family altar, lead us in the hymn of praise and in pouring out the soul to God. He is in a more endeared, a happier and holier sphere, enjoying the smiles and presence of his God and Redeemer. Pray for me that I may have grace to follow his example as he followed Christ, and at last to unite in his songs."

The above pages have sufficiently shown in what varied forms he rendered himself useful, as the *teacher of a day school;* in the relations he sustained to the *Sabbath school* cause, and to the *Tract* cause; in *Bible classes,* and in religious meetings; to families and to individuals. The variety of efforts he made with his *pen* is equally striking. Not only did he address moving appeals to individuals; but if a thought occurred which he judged to be of general interest, he embodied it in a few paragraphs and sent it for insertion in some religious paper; and even if he inserted a scrap in an album, he improved the opportunity to direct the reader's mind to Christ.

In the *Temperance cause* he enlisted with a whole heart as early as 1823; rejecting all that could intoxicate, including tobacco in all its forms, and throwing an influence in a thousand ways to extend the Temperance reformation.

Many *pious young men* were by him sought out and directed towards the Ministry.

To the *cause of Missions,* both in our own and pagan lands, he was steadfastly devoted. He not only turned his eye away from the *accumulation of property* as the object of his life; but felt the duty and claimed the blessedness to his own soul, of imparting for the cause of Christ a portion of what he had. On his dying bed, he mentioned to Mrs. Page, that five dollars, which before his sickness he had subscribed to a benevolent object, remained unpaid. "We have consecrated it to God," said he, "and I had rather it would be paid. You had better pay it, and trust him."

His familiarity with the character and religious bearing of all the Society's publications, and with the general state and wants of the community, rendered him skillful in selecting publications appropriate to the different fields and circumstances for which they were designed; and also in giving an impulse and a wise direction to the feelings and efforts of Christians who were continually calling for the transaction of business.

And in all, it abundantly appears that he felt that the efficiency was alone with God; and mingled continual prayer for *the gift of gifts*—the accompanying influences of the Holy Spirit.

Is it wonderful that GOD SHOULD BLESS his efforts? That, in each church with which he stood connected, individuals, when relating their religious experience, should be heard referring to his faithful endeavors as the means of bringing them to Christ? That a revenue of souls should have been gathered from the place of his nativity; *thirty-two* teachers be brought publicly to profess Christ, from one of his Sabbath schools, and *nine* of them have set their faces toward the Ministry? That *thirty-four* souls should hopefully have been gathered by him and his fellow-laborers from one ward of the city; and *fifty-eight*, in connection with his efforts and those of a few endeared associates, have been brought to join themselves to the people of God, from the Tract and Bible houses? That individuals should come to his dying bed, and thank him with tears for his fidelity to their own souls?

Is it wonderful, that, in speaking to her who is now his widow, of his early departure, and looking back on his work on earth as ended, he should, with the solemnity of eternity on his countenance, say: "I know it is all of God's grace, and nothing that I have done; but I think I have had evidence that *more than one hundred souls have been converted to God* through my own direct and personal instrumentality."

Look at the influence of such a Christian life *on a large scale*. Suppose every Christian labored, I do not say with such talents, but with such *a heart to the work*. Suppose there were *ten* such Christians in every evangelical church throughout our land, and God should equally bless their labors. How would they rouse their fellow Christians to duty. How would they search the highways and hedges, and by God's grace compel the ungodly to come in. How would they instruct the rising age. How would they hold up the hands of faithful ministers. How would the Holy Spirit be shed down in answer to their prayers. How would their influence penetrate through every vein of this great community; and how soon would living piety here pour its influence on every benighted land. Such a light as would then shine could not be hid. It would illumine the world, and Christ would come and possess the nations.

CHAPTER 10

TRIUMPHS OF GRACE ON HIS DYING BED.

It remains only to linger a little while with our brother in the chamber of death. We did not look to his dying bed for *evidence* of his good estate. This we had in his life. Nor have we to record what occurred in the hurry, and excitement, and delirium of dying. He was let down to the grave by a gradual process of four months; and, contrary to almost all example, gave up all expectation of living many weeks before he left us, and while in the full and perfect exercise of his mental powers.

It cannot be said, that death had to him no terrors. This enemy did not come and steal him away unawares; nor were the powers of his mind blunted by disease, or medicine. The king of terrors presented himself as if he would *challenge Divine grace* to gain a victory. He showed him usefulness closed; a dependent widow and children, agonizing bodily pain, and his soul about to appear before God.

His disease was in the vital organs, and a continual cough gave alarming evidence that it was seating itself upon the lungs. About six weeks previous to his death, Dr. W——, one of the skillful and pious physicians who gave him their gratuitous counsel and aid, made a careful examination with the stethoscope; and, as a faithful friend, informed him that his lungs were ulcerated, and he must die. "He received the announcement," says the physician, "calmly; as a man who felt that it is a solemn thing to exchange worlds, but that he had a *home in heaven."*

To a heart so spiritually alive, the scene before him was unutterably solemn and momentous. He wished clear evidence of his union to Christ, that should leave no question of his interest in him; and to have *a constant and lively sense of his immediate presence*. Nothing short of this could meet the urgency of his case; and this, for some days, he did not attain.

"About six weeks before his death," says a kind brother who called on him with a Christian friend, "we found him in much mental distress. He said he had been endeavoring to examine his past life, but it was all a blank. 'O,' said he, 'I have done nothing for Christ. What an unprofitable life have I lived! How can one be a Christian who has done no more to prevent his acquaintance, and even his own household, from going down to hell.' We repeated to him a number of Scripture promises. He said they were precious promises, but he could not appropriate them to himself."

"A few days after," says the same brother, "we called on him again; and found that the desire of his heart was granted. Christ was with him; and his emphatic language was, 'It seems as if I never knew before what it was to love him.' He appeared to feel that he had obtained *a new view* of the love of Christ, which he was anxious to communicate for our benefit. 'I have been following him,' he said, 'all along as the evangelists record his history—how he healed the sick—how he fed the hungry—cast out devils—comforted the sorrowful—and at last *died for poor sinners*'—(when his weeping prevented utterance)—'O who can help loving such a blessed Savior!'

"'I think I have evidence of love to Christ,' he soon added, 'from another source; I *love his people*. O how my heart goes out towards all the dear brethren who love Christ, and are trying to save poor sinners from hell. Brother A——, and brother B——, and brother ——; O that the Lord will make them more faithful, and more useful. Do, brethren,' said he to us, 'be faithful to souls. It will be time enough to rest by and by.'"

Again he said: "Should I go into a meeting and see a Christian with his eyes filled with tears, and his heart glowing with love to souls, pleading with sinners to come to Christ and live, should not I love him? And when Christ comes and weeps over poor sinners, and says, 'O Jerusalem, Jerusalem, how often would I have gathered thy children together, even as a hen gathered her chickens under her wings, and ye would not!'—shan't I love him? I know I love that Christian brother that would feel so; and don't I love Christ? I do love him. I do love him."

The cloud returned no more till his spirit took its upward flight.

The writer having been some time absent from the city, sat by his bedside alone, expecting it might be the last interview with him on earth, when the following conversation, almost word for word occurred.

"I have thought a great deal of you in my absence, brother Page; and when I come here and find you so low, it is very affecting. How wonderfully God is dealing with us. He has seen fit to take away both of my children; you are sinking; and your son, by falling from an upper window, has very narrowly escaped death."

"Yes," he replied, in slow, feeble and tender tones, "God mingles mercies with afflictions. I want to thank him for preserving Cyrus' life. It is a great mercy."

"It is wonderful," I added, "that God often cuts down those who seem most needed. Brother Hunter is gone; Evarts and Cornelius are gone. He makes great breaches on the church."

"O, brother H——," said he, (as if he could not bear the allusion to himself as having been specially useful,) "I am nothing; and have done nothing. I'm nothing but a poor sinner. I'm a blank, and less than a blank. I hang on the mere merits of Christ."

"Has it not been a great trial to give up your wife and children, and all your work here?"

"It has been a trial to give them up; but not my great trial. I wanted a clear sense of the presence of Christ in my heart. For some time I could not get a clear view of him; and it was not till I followed him all along from the manger to the cross, that I seemed to get a clear view of him as just the Savior I need, and bring him home to my heart. I've given all up here. My work here is *all done*—its *all done*. What I want now is a sense of the presence of Christ; and I think he is with me, and sustains me."

"I rejoice that it is so; and may his grace carry you through. I want before you die to thank you, brother Page, for your uniform kindness during the nine years we have been laboring together; and especially for the help you have given me in the spiritual life."

"O, brother H——, don't thank me. I've done nothing, and been nothing but a poor miserable sinner. I don't want any thanks."

"I have always felt," I added, "that you have essentially aided me in the Christian course."

"Ah, I've often felt wrong, and done wrong. I want you, brother H——, to forgive all you have seen amiss."

"I have nothing to forgive. I wish rather to confess my faults to you."

"O, don't speak of it, brother H——, I've come short in every thing"—(bursting into a flood of tears.)

The scene was full of instruction. I could scarcely avoid the impression that I was conversing with his spirit already purified for heaven. To see one who had lived such a life thus abasing himself; to see him shudder at the intimation that he had been specially useful; to hear him say, amid the solemnities of dying, "I am nothing, and have done nothing; I'm a blank, and less than a blank; I have done wrong and felt wrong, and cast my soul alone on the blood and righteousness of Christ"—opened *a new view of heaven;* and made me feel, that, whoever arrives at that blessed abode—whatever his life has been, however much he has labored for Christ and the souls of men,—will THERE PROSTRATE HIMSELF LOWER THAN THE DUST, AND GIVE TO GOD ALL, ALL THE GLORY, FOR EVER AND EVER.

"You must feel some anxiety for your wife and children. I will endeavor to do what I can for them."

"I don't want any promises. God will take care of them."

"I have hoped, that it will be in the hearts of friends around us to contribute something for them."

"It can't be expected that any thing like what would support them could be raised. But *I give all that up.*"

"I understand you have expressed a desire that your body be removed to Coventry. If so, I hope I may accompany it."

"Ah, I've no concern about this poor body. All will be done right about it."

About this time, a friend from his native place visited him; and asking if he had any message for his parents and friends, he said, "Yes.

"Tell my aged parents not to despond because God has taken me first; for he will be their stay and support, and soon we shall meet where parting will be no more.

"Tell ——, that it will be hard dying without an interest in Christ.

"Tell sister L——, I expect soon to meet her in heaven.

"Tell my former pastor, that I remember with gratitude the instructions received from his lips."

On the following Sabbath, as the writer called on him, he said: "I wanted to have *gone home* today; but they're trying to keep me here. My work here is *all done*, and I want to be with Christ."

"Do you not look back now with peculiar pleasure on your direct personal efforts for the good of souls?"

"I look upon *personal conversation and prayer with individuals* as among my most successful endeavours, and hope I have done some good. But it is not me. It's all of grace in Christ. There's nothing in me but sin. I'm nothing—nothing—less than nothing. Brother H——, I have been a great sinner."

"Is it the sins of your heart that trouble you chiefly?"

"Not particularly. I've been a great sinner in my childhood—and youth—and all my life—the chief of sinners. But, 'it is a faithful saying, and worthy of all acceptation, that Christ Jesus came into the world to save sinners.'"

"Do you feel that it is your choice now to go?"

"Yes, if it is God's will."

"Should he please to restore you, would you not be willing to remain here and labor a little longer?"

"O yes, I think so, if it was his will. But my work on earth is *all done*. I want now to go and be with Christ. Prophets, and apostles, and martyrs are there; and many pious friends are there—I feel that I should like to meet them. Christ will be there; and we shall be like him, and see him as he is: that will be enough."

"Is it not wonderful that Christians do not live in a nearer view of death?"

"O yes; I'm a wonder to myself. I didn't feel how short this life is."

Some time previous to this conversation, he had adjusted all his earthly concerns; reviewed his will; arranged his papers; given advice respecting his family and his burial; and thenceforward he seemed to feel that his work here was "all done," and to welcome nothing that did not immediately pertain to the exchange of worlds. The daily paper had for weeks been put aside as having "nothing of Christ in it," though not without expressing his belief that ere long the daily papers shall carry to their readers messages of salvation; and when his family were reading to him from religious papers, he would sometimes stop them, saying, "Is there any thing there for a dying man? If so, read it."

He relished nothing but what was *eminently spiritual;* and regretted that he had not treasured more of the Bible in his memory. The twenty-third Psalm and the last chapter of the Revelation were very precious to him. At one time he said, "Do read me a spiritual hymn, or something from the Bible: I'm starving." Again, as a clergyman came in, he said, "Do look out some hymns that express a great deal of heaven. Many of the hymns seem tame. They are pretty poetry, but do not present the joys of redemption and the glory of Christ. When I have a clear view of Christ, my fears vanish, and I can trust myself wholly in his hands."

It was remarked by those most familiar at his bedside, that not one impenitent acquaintance visited him, whom he did not seem to have warned. The tenor of his language to them was: "I have said all I can say. I can now add nothing new. My work here is all done."

Finding that his life was continued longer than he expected, he said: "I thought my work was done; but I find it is not. I must strive to urge Christians and sinners to duty from this dying bed."

As two brethren of the church from which he had recently separated himself came in, he said: "You will allow me to speak freely as a dying man. Are the dear brethren of the church awake? Are they laboring for souls? If I were to be raised up from this dying bed, would you not feel that *I* ought to be faithful? And is the duty less *yours* than it would be *mine?*"

More than once he said, "The millennium will never come until Christians are more awake to duty." And again, "O for a holy Ministry! a Ministry devoted to the salvation of souls! I can't bear to have *so much time wasted in controversy.* If all would devote themselves to the salvation of souls, how many might be saved from eternal burnings."

The principal of a large female school coming in, he entreated her to be faithful to the souls of her pupils; and urged the momentous consequences, should they be converted to God. She was much affected, and begged him to pray for her, when he immediately offered a short, appropriate prayer for her and all committed to her charge.

He observed that the number of the impenitent who visited him was comparatively small; and when one with whom he had conversed, retired, he said, "O how the impenitent dread a dying bed!"

As a Christian friend, on seeing him so much reduced, expressed his regret that he left the church with which he had been so long connected, for the new enterprise, he said: "There were motives pressing upon me that I could not resist. I felt that one at least of the officers of that church ought to go; and hard as it was to tear myself away from the dear brethren, I do not regret it. There are some praying souls there, and I feel that God will bless their efforts for that destitute part of the city."

His *utterance in disturbed sleep* continually indicated what the burden of his life had been. Generally, it was prayer, or an appeal to Christians, or the impenitent.

—— "No more *pain*—no more *sin*," (was once his unconscious utterance.) "Lord, reveal thyself to us. Show us thy glory."

At another time he exclaimed with great earnestness: "Dear brethren! *where are you?* WHERE ARE YOU? Are you in the light of God's countenance? Are you in the light of the Sun of Righteousness?"

Again, as if he were addressing the impenitent: "'*Now* is the accepted time; *now* is the day of salvation.' O why will you not turn and give your hearts to God? Why will you go down to hell?"

Again he said, with melting tenderness, as if some effort of his had been unavailing: "Poor girl! she has rejected her Savior, and her soul must be lost."

The visit of J—— H—— T——, his fellow-laborer in the Tract and Bible houses, was peculiarly gratifying. He greeted him on being so near home; they conversed on the dealings of the Lord with them, and the glories of eternity; and bade one another farewell for *a little while*, till they should meet again never to separate.

Again he said: "A death-bed is a precious place, when we have the presence of Christ—then to wake to a glorious immortality. God does not send one unnecessary affliction."

Again: "I feel as if I had got half-way home. I cannot bear to stop. It would be a pity to have the flesh return on these limbs again."

Perhaps SACRED MUSIC was never a source of more spiritual benefit or enjoyment in the chamber of sickness and death. For some years he led the devotions of the sanctuary, and in his earlier days was accustomed to play on the bass-viol and the flute. In his latter years, he made singing *strictly a devotional exercise:* a point, the practical bearing of which on the Christian life cannot be too much urged. He used it as such at social meetings, and uniformly made it a part of family worship. Providence kindly so ordered it, that Mr. F. a Christian brother, accustomed to lead choirs in the city, resided near, who, to his love of music, joined a tender sympathy with the sick and dying. At the request of Mr. Page he sung a few appropriate selections; and finding they were as a precious balm to his heart, tendered his services to come in daily and as often as he desired. The impression made upon the mind of the dying man was so strong, that he would anticipate his return with great interest. "I expect Mr. F. soon," he would say to his family, "and I want you all to be here." When he arrived, he would inquire for each absent member, unwilling that the singing should commence till all were present; and then anxious that all should join in the praises of the Most High. After singing one day, he said: "How sweet—and if the music of earth is so sweet, what must be the music of heaven, where all the heavenly hosts unite their voices—ten thousand upon ten thousand!"

The beautiful hymns, "Rock of Ages," and "My Faith Looks up to Thee," as set to music in the "Spiritual Songs," took precedence of all others. The music of the first was composed by Mr. Hastings, of New York, and of the other by Mr. L. Mason, of Boston, who have consented to their insertion here, as it may be gratifying to some readers, and perhaps be the means of adding consolation to some other departing friend.

The hymn beginning "How sweet the name of Jesus sounds," as set to music in the same work, was also peculiarly precious to him, and one that he often repeated. At one time he asked for the reading of the hymn, "When languor and disease invade," etc. and as the fifth verse was read, said with emphasis, "Yes,

> "Sweet to lie passive in his hands,
> "And know no will but his."

On one occasion, as they were singing from the 17th Psalm, beginning with the words,

> "What sinners value I resign,

"he repeated the verses," says one who was present, "with a tone and animation more than earthly:

> "'Lord, 'tis enough that Thou art mine:

(Continued on page 124.)

MY FAITH LOOKS UP TO THEE

My faith looks up to thee, Thou Lamb of Cal-va - ry;

Savior   divine!   Now hear me   while   I   pray;   Take all my

guilt   away;   O let me   from this day   Be   whol - ly   thine.

My faith looks up to thee,
Thou Lamb of Calvary;
   Savior divine!
Now hear me while I pray;
Take all my guilt away;
O let me from this day
   Be wholly thine.

May thy rich grace impart
Strength to my fainting heart,
   My zeal inspire;
As thou hast died for me,
O may my love to thee,
Pure, warm, and changeless be,
   A living fire.

While life's dark maze I tread,
And griefs around me spread
   Be thou my guide;
Bid darkness turn to day,
Wipe sorrow's tears away,
Nor let me ever stray
   From thee aside.

When ends life's transient dream
When death's cold sullen stream
   Shall o'er me roll;
Blest Savior, then in love,
Fear and distrust remove;
O bear me safe above—
   A ransom'd soul.

ROCK OF AGES

Rock of ages, cleft for me,
Let me hide myself in thee;
Let the water and the blood,
From thy wounded side that flow'd,
Be of sin the perfect cure,
Save me, Lord, and make me pure.

Should my tears for ever flow;
Should my zeal no languor know;
This for sin could not atone;
Thou must save, and thou alone.
In my hand no price I bring;
Simply to thy cross I cling.

While I draw this fleeting breath,
When mine eyelids close in death,
When I rise to worlds unknown,
And behold thee on thy throne—
Rock of Ages, cleft for me,
Let me hide myself in thee.

"'I shall behold thy blissful face,
"'And stand complete in righteousness.'"

As he repeated the 5th verse, with inexpressible ardor and solemnity, we felt almost that we were already transported to those blissful regions:

"'O GLORIOUS HOUR! O BLEST ABODE!
"'*I shall be near*, and LIKE MY GOD.'"

"I wonder," he said, "that singing is not more used around the bed of the sick. It seems to me admirably adapted to cheer and comfort them."

He expressed an earnest desire that all his family should learn to sing. "Then," said he, "you can have a little heaven here below."

Again he said: "O how can the churches be so indifferent to the praises of the sanctuary—the very employment of heaven! how can Christians sing so little in their families—it is the beginning of heaven—it is heaven on earth."

As he was apparently slumbering, his infant son struck the strings of a bass viol that stood in the room—"My little son," said he, "is that you? Do that again. Pa loves to hear that."

On hearing an organ as it passed in the street he said: "That sounds sweet. I am becoming very fond of instrumental music: I suppose there will be a good deal of it from the golden harps of heaven."

At one time, with much effort, he sung the line, "Rise, my soul, and stretch thy wings;" but not having strength to proceed, stopped, saying, "O when shall I go *home?* How long must I be burdened with this body! The Lord knows how much suffering I need to prepare me for his kingdom."

In all his sickness, he exhibited surprising *tenderness of spirit.* He could not bear the thought that there were any Christians who did not love one another, and who were not engaged in the service of Christ. If he had manifested the least *impatience*, he would pray God to forgive him; beg his wife to forgive him; and often express his gratitude for the kindness he received, in the most affecting manner. Frequently he wept in view of the long continued and gratuitous attentions of his stated physician, (Dr. J. C. B.) As he had been ministering to his necessities one day, and had led in prayer, and retired, he said with tears: "How good to have some one to carry you up into heaven!" adding, after a pause, "When I think of his prolonged and unwearied kindness to us, my heart swells with emotions which I cannot utter."

He was continually endeavoring to relieve the sorrows of those around him. When he saw her weeping, who was soon to be a widow, he summoned his utmost efforts, and urged his most ardent supplications to God, that she might have Divine consolation; and when he found that she had yielded the point, and given him, and herself, and her children, and her all away to God, to be disposed of according to his pleasure, he expressed great joy and gratitude. "God will take care of you," said he, "I am sure of it. Only trust in God, and he will provide for you. His promises to the widow and the fatherless are precious. The Bible is full of them."

His *tender dread of sin* continued to the last. A dear Christian friend says, he regards the night he watched with him, as one of the most privileged seasons of his life. They had many short and delightful interviews. Towards morning he spoke very seriously: "Have you seen any thing, brother, in which you think I have *sinned* tonight?" "Nothing in particular," was the reply. "Twice," added the faithful affectionate brother, "you spoke of the pain occasioned by your labored respiration, and perhaps expressed a little impatience." He immediately lifted up his tearful eye to God, and offered an earnest prayer, that he might he purified from *all* sin.

After violent coughing, he said, "My children, you see this is suffering. It is for *sin.*"

At another time he said: "The Bible speaks of perfection. I feel no perfection. I am all sin. Christ is perfect, and his blood cleanseth from all sin."

Again he said, "Sometimes I so earnestly desire to depart, I feel as though I could not wait; but I want you to persuade me not to feel so. I fear it is wrong."

Equally undiminished was his *sense of his unworthiness.* As one, now a brother in the church, had wept at his bedside, and thanked him for his faithful efforts in arresting him in his downward course of sin, he said: "I know not what to do with such scenes—there's a great deal too much ascribed to man."

His eldest son having been absent, he expressed a great desire to see him before he died; and when he arrived, clasped him for many minutes in his withered arms, and bestowed upon him a father's richest counsels and blessing. This had been, for some time, the only remaining earthly favor he had had to request. He wished to have all his children once more together, and to give them his dying counsels.

A few days before he died, after a paroxysm of coughing, he said: "I was in hopes to depart; but I must wait a little longer. How long probably before another ulcer will fill? O, when shall I awake in Thy likeness!"

Again he repeated the words, "Home! home!" and prayed: "O for a free and full discharge. Lord Jesus, come quickly. Why wait thy chariot wheels so long? I dedicate myself to thee. O may I have the victory. O come quickly. Come, Lord Jesus, come quickly."

A little before his death, as all his family were around him, after a short prayer, in weakness and want of breath that rendered utterance scarcely possible, he addressed a word to each. "I want you all," said he, "to be a bundle of love."

To Mrs. Page. "Though a thousand miles apart, you may be serving God here—and I in heaven."

To his eldest son. "I want you should be *a holy man*—an active, living Christian."

To his daughter. "Stand fast. Be steadfast in the faith. Wander not from God. Be wholly his."

To a younger son. "O be a Christian indeed, my son."

To the infant. "Love God. Learn what he is—what heaven is."

To a niece. "I have been committing all my family to God. Love God. Pray to him daily."

Then he prayed: "I thank thee for suffering. I deserve it. How much I deserved death—eternal death! Deliver me from a long series of sufferings, if consistent; but I submit. Let me not complain nor dictate. Remember thine handmaiden. Remember her in her trials. Thou knowest the supports she needs—grant them fully. May she be willing to commit me to thy hands. Bless this daughter, and all these children, and all their concerns. I COMMIT MYSELF TO THEE, JESUS, SAVIOR OF SINNERS. O THE INFINITE LOVE OF CHRIST! I MAY STOP MY MOUTH, AND LIE IN THE DUST."

This is the legacy he left to a lonely widow, and four fatherless children.

This his testimony to the *matchless grace of God*, abounding, through Christ, to one who had no merits of his own.

This his moving persuasive *to every child of God* to abound in duty.

This his voice of warning and entreaty *to rebel sinners*, saying, "Be ye reconciled to God."

The mercy and kindness of a covenant God, to whom he committed his family with such implicit trust, claims here to be recorded in the fact, that soon after his death, a few Christian friends assembled, and commenced a subscription for the benefit of the widow and children, which was raised to $2,000. As the subject was mentioned to a pious mechanic, he said, with the tear standing in his eye: "I want to give something. Here are ten dollars. But for Mr. Page, I should probably have sunk into a miserable eternity." He was asked to relate the circumstances, and thus replied.

"On New Year's Day, 1827 or 8, which was Monday, I reflected that I had never attended a monthly concert of prayer in this city, and determined that for once I would go. I went early, found only the sexton in the room, and sat down. Soon there came in a plain man, who spoke very pleasantly to the sexton, and then coming and sitting by my side, after a kind salutation, said: 'I trust you love the Savior?' The question instantly filled my eyes with tears. *I had been preached to,* AT ARMS' LENGTH, *all my days in New Hampshire; but this was the first time in my life that ever a Christian thus kindly and directly put such a question to my heart.* We conversed considerably together, in the course of which, at his request, I gave him my name and residence. *The next day he came into my shop,* and brought me the Tract 'Way to be Saved,' which he thought I should like to read. He called again and again. I became interested in him, and the next Sabbath joined his Sabbath school; was brought, as I hope, to Christ, and soon united with the church."

The body of Mr. Page, according to a suggestion above, was removed to Coventry, his native place, and over his grave a marble slab bears the following epitaph:

"𝕴𝖓 𝕸𝖊𝖒𝖔𝖗𝖕 𝖔𝖋

"HARLAN PAGE,

"FOR NINE YEARS DEPOSITARY OF THE

"American Tract Society,

"WHO DIED AT NEW YORK,

"September 23, 1834,

"IN THE TRIUMPH OF FAITH,

"Aged 43.

"He 'ceased not to warn every one night and day with tears.'"

Made in the USA
Las Vegas, NV
12 January 2024

84279983R00080